IMPROVED MASONIC RITUAL AND MONITOR

JANUARY 5, 2019
INTELLECTUAL SOLUTIONS
nammubenavraham@gmail.com

1

ACTIVE 33°

SOUTHERN JURISDICTION

HONORARY 33°

HONORARY 33°

NORTHERN JURISDICTION

ROYAL ORDER OF SCOTLAND

KNIGHT COMMANDER
OF THE
COURT OF HONOR

ORDER OF KNIGHTS TEMPLAR
COMMANDERY

A.A.O.N.M.S.

SUBLIME PRINCE
OF THE ROYAL SECRET

SHRINE

31 — GRAND INSPECTOR INQUISITOR COMMANDER
30 — KNIGHT KADOSH
29 — KNIGHT OF ST. ANDREW
28 — KNIGHT OF THE SUN
27 — KNIGHT COMMANDER OF THE TEMPLE
26 — PRINCE OF MERCY
25 — KNIGHT of the BRAZEN SERPENT
24 — PRINCE OF THE TABERNACLE
23 — CHIEF OF THE TABERNACLE
22 — KNIGHT OF THE ROYAL AXE
21 — NOACHITE OR PRUSSIAN KNIGHT
20 — GRAND MASTER OF ALL SYMBOLIC LODGES
19 — GRAND PONTIFF
18 — KNIGHT OF THE ROSE CROIX
17 — KNIGHTS OF THE EAST & WEST
16 — PRINCE OF JERUSALEM
15 — KNIGHT of the EAST OR SWORD
14 — GRAND ELECT MASON
13 — MASTER OF THE NINTH ARCH
12 — GRAND MASTER ARCHITECT
11 — SUBLIME MASTER ELECTED
10 — MASTER ELECT OF FIFTEEN
9 — MASTER ELECT OF NINE
8 — INTENDANT of the BUILDINGS
7 — PROVOST & JUDGE
6 — INTIMATE SECRETARY
5 — PERFECT MASTER
4 — SECRET MASTER

CONSISTORIAL DEGREE
CHAPTER
COUNCIL
LODGE OF PERFECTION

ORDER OF
KNIGHTS OF MALTA

COUNCIL

SUPER EXCELLENT MASTER

SELECT MASTER 9

ROYAL MASTER 8

ORDER OF THE
RED CROSS

ROYAL ARCH MASON

CHAPTER

MOST EXCELLENT MASTER

TALL CEDARS
OF LEBANON

GROTTO
MOVPER

PAST MASTER (VIRTUAL)

MARK MASTER

YORK RITE

MASTER MASON

SCOTTISH RITE

FELLOW CRAFT

ENTERED APPRENTICE
BLUE LODGE

ORDER OF WHITE SHRINE

ORDER OF EASTERN STAR

ORDER OF THE AMARANTH

U.S.A. Only
Council
Super Excellent Master
Select Master
Royal Master
Tall Cedars of Lebanon
Past Master (Virtual)
Knight Commander of the
Court of Honor
Order of the Amaranth

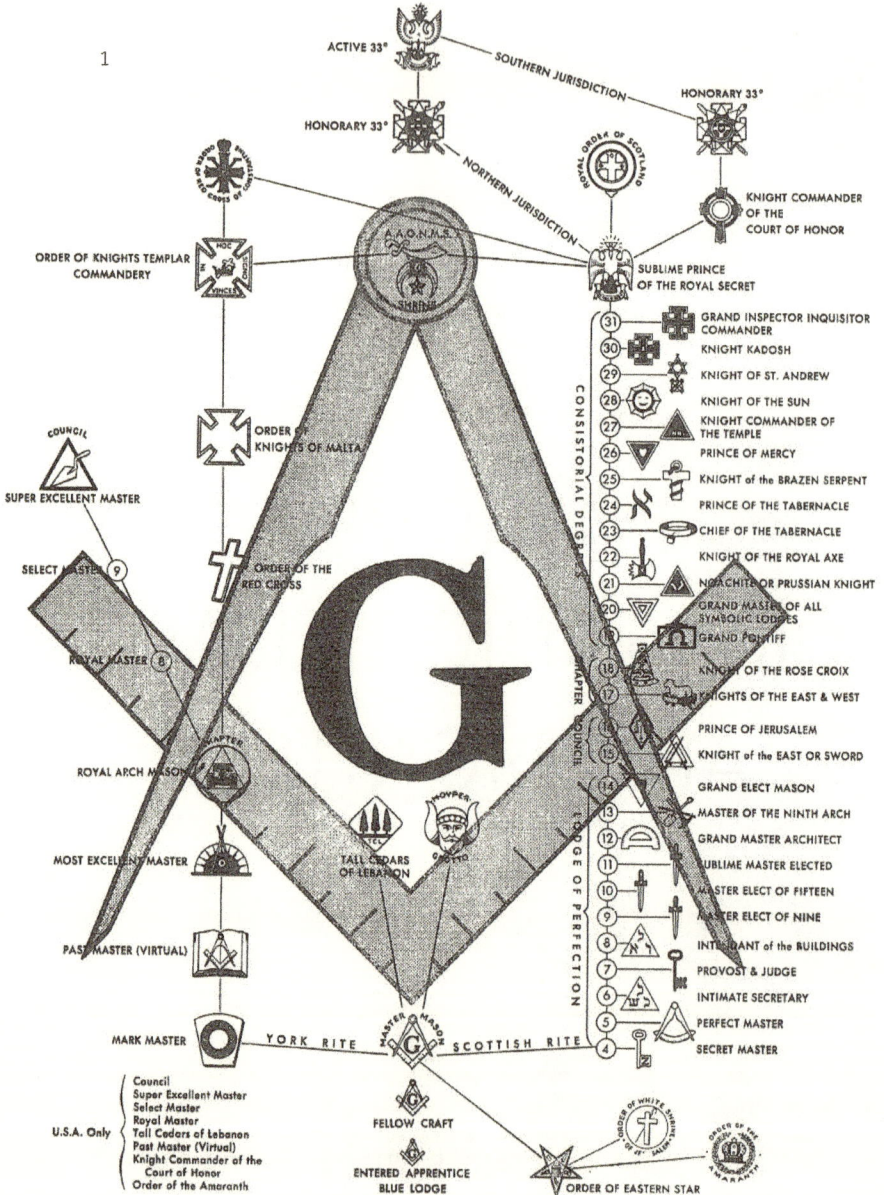

¹ Layout of the masonic system from the symbolic lodge and beyond

LODGE JEWELS.

PAST MASTER.

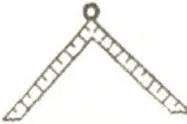

MASTER.

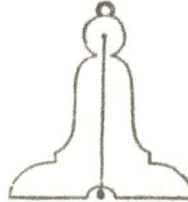

SENIOR WARDEN.

JUNIOR WARDEN.

TREASURER.

SECRETARY.

SENIOR DEACON.

JUNIOR DEACON.

STEWARDS.

MASTERS OF CEREMONIES.

TILER.

48

219

Foreword

The Improved Masonic Ritual and Monitor is a must-have for every mason. While it provides insight into the masonic system the inner workings of the lodge is preserved and not revealed in this work. The goal of the Improved Masonic Ritual and Monitor is to provide historical information about the honorable fraternity of Freemasonry. It is not intended to provide the esoteric knowledge of its philosophy.

Though information can be printed on pages the spirit of Freemasonry can only be imbued upon its member within a lodge. We maintain that the light of freemasonry is not a secret in and of itself. Without an upright heart the reader will not understand masonic literature and likewise will not misuse what he does not understand.

To the readers who remember where you were first made a mason and what makes you a mason and this work will be one of the guiding lights to assist you in developing along your masonic journey. "Know Thyself and you will understand GAOTU."

ENTERED APPRENTICE, OR FIRST DEGREE

[2]*Seven Freemasons, viz., six Entered Apprentices and one Master Mason, acting under a charter or dispensation from some Grand Lodge, is the requisite number to constitute a Lodge of Masons, and to initiate a candidate to the First Degree of Masonry.*

[3]*They assemble in a room well-guarded from all cowans and eavesdroppers, in the second or third story (as the case may be) of some building suitably prepared and furnished*

---

[2] A body of mason is herein explained. Seven Mason of varying degrees are required to open an E.A. lodge. This body of masons must have a charter from a grand body allowing it to work.

[3] A location is selected based upon exposure to those who do not have the masonic rights to be a part of a masonic lodge. Infiltration of the order is of great importance and privacy of the rights and rituals of the order are protected by the solemn commitments of its members.

for Lodge purposes, which is, by Masons, termed "the Ground Floor of King Solomon's Temple."

The officers take their seats, as represented in the Plate on page 8. [4]Lodge-meetings are arranged as follows, viz.: a "regular" is held but once a month (i.e. every month on, or preceding, the full of the moon in each month); special meetings are held as often as the exigency of the case may seem to demand, if every night in the week, Sunday excepted. If Tuesday should be Lodge night, by Masons it would be termed, "Tuesday evening on or before the full of the moon, a regular night."

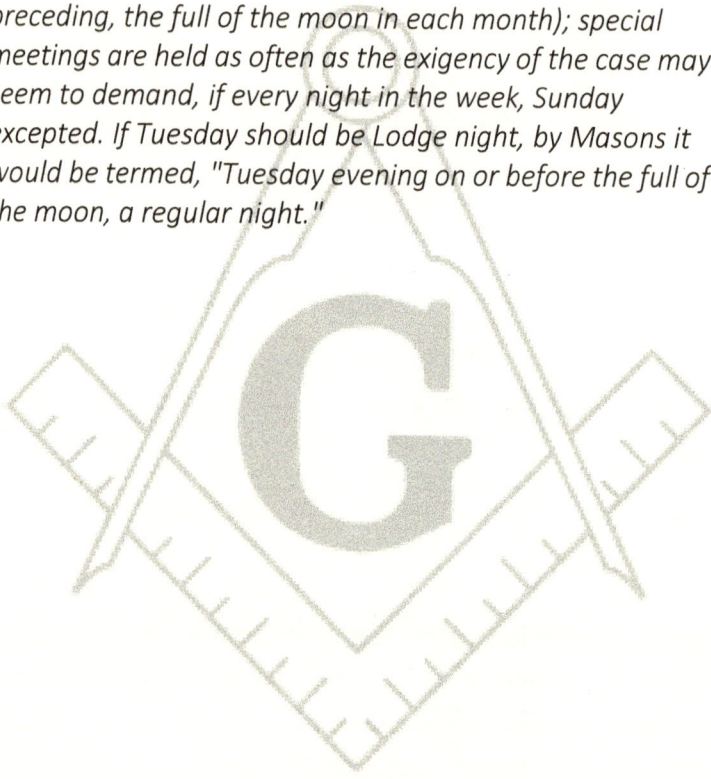

---

[4] Meeting times vary based upon the by-laws of a lodge. Members of a lodge decide where and when meetings will take place.

[5]LODGE OF ENTERED APPRENTICES, FELLOW CRAFTS, OR MASTER MASONS.

1. Candidate prays. 2. First stop. 3. Second stop. 4. Third stop. 5. Room where candidates are prepared. 6. Anteroom where members enter the lodge. 7. Hall. 8. Doors. 9. Door through which candidates are admitted into the lodge. 10. Door through which members enter. 11. Altar. 12. Treasurer. 13. Secretary. 14. Senior Deacon. 15. Worshipful Master. 16. Junior Warden. 17 and 18. Stewards. 19. Senior Warden. 20. Junior Deacon. 21. Tyler.

[6]All business relative to Masonry is done at a "regular," and in the Third, or Master Mason Degree. None but Master Masons are allowed to be present at such meetings; balloting for candidates is done on a "regular," also receiving petitions, committee reports, &c., &c.

[7]A petition for the degrees of Masonry is received at a "regular" (though, as a common thing, Grand Lodges of each State make such arrangements as they may deem best for the regulation of their several subordinate Lodges).

---

[5] The lodge is arranged in a matter that is consistent with Masonic law. See layout for details. The W.M. is always seated in the east of the lodge, the Senior Warden in the West, and the Junior Warden in the South.

[6] The meetings are styled business meetings. This denotes a certain part of a meeting of mason at which time administrative responsibilities of the lodge and its member are addressed.

[7] A petition is an application to a lodge from a prospective candidate. A candidate must petition a lodge for membership and be accepted by the members to be admitted in the Order of Freemasonry.

[8]At the time of receiving a petition for the degrees of Masonry, the Master appoints a committee of three, whose duty it is to make inquiry after the character of the applicant, and report good or bad, as the case may be, at the next regular meeting, when it is acted upon by the Lodge.

Upon reception of the committee's report, a ballot is had: if no black balls appear, the candidate is declared duly elected; but if one black ball or more appear, he is declared rejected.

[9]No business is done in a Lodge of Entered Apprentices, except to initiate a candidate to the First Degree in Masonry, nor is any business done in a Fellow Crafts' Lodge, except to pass a Fellow Craft from the first to the second degree. To explain more thoroughly: when a candidate is initiated to the First Degree, he is styled as "entered;" when he has taken the Second Degree, "passed." and when he has taken the Third, "raised" to the sublime Degree of a Master Mason. No one is allowed to be present, in any degree of Masonry, except he be one of that same degree or higher. The Master always wears his hat when presiding as such, but no other officer, in a "Blue Lodge" (a "Blue Lodge" is a Lodge of Master Masons, where only three degrees are conferred, viz.: Entered Apprentice, 1st; Fellow Craft, 2d; Master Mason, 3d. Country Lodges are mostly all "Blue Lodges").

---

[8] A committee is assigned to investigate the candidate. The W.M. will determine who the members of the committee will be.
[9] No business is done in an E.A lodge however degree work is performed during this time.

A Lodge of Fellow Craft Masons consists of five, viz.:
Worshipful Master, Senior and Junior Wardens, Senior and
Junior Dear hens; yet seven besides Tyler assist and take
their seats as in the Entered Apprentice's Degree. Masons
style the Fellow Craft Lodge "the Middle Chamber of King
Solomon's Temple."

Three Master Masons is the requisite number to constitute
a Masters' Lodge, which is called by Masons "the Sanctum
Sanctorum, or Holy of Holies of King Solomon's Temple."
Although there are all that is required by "Masonic Law" to
open a Third-Degree Lodge, there are seven besides the
Tyler, as in the other degrees.

All the Lodges meet in one room, alike furnished, for the
conferring of the different degrees (E. A., F. C., and M. M.);
but they are masonically styled by the Craft as the Ground
Floor, Middle Chamber, and Sanctum Sanctorum.

A person being in the room, while open on the First Degree,
would not see any difference in the appearance of the room
from a Master Masons' Lodge. It is the duty of Tyler to
inform all the brethren to what degree the Lodge is at
work, especially those that arrive too late (i.e., after the
Lodge has been opened). so that none will be liable to give
the wrong sign to the Worshipful Master when he enters. If
the Lodge is opened on the First Degree, there he present
those who had taken only one degree, and, if the brother
arriving late should be ignorant of this fact, and make a
Third-Degree sign, they would see it;

caution on
should
given to
by the
entering

consequently,
this point
always be
such brethren
Tyler, before
the Lodge.

[11]Usual way: Brethren that arrive too late come up to the ante-room, which they find occupied by the Tyler, sword in hand; after inquiring of the Tyler on what degree the Lodge is at work (opened), they put on an apron, and request the Tyler to let them in; the Tyler steps to the door, gives one rap (•), i.e. if opened on the First Degree; two raps (• •), if Second Degree; three raps (• • •), if the Third Degree; which being heard by the Junior Deacon, on the inside, he reports to the Master the alarm, as follows, viz.:

J. D.--Worshipful Master, there is an alarm at the inner door of our Lodge.

---

[10] Worshipful Master

[11] Members that are late for the meeting will be required to address the lodge in the appropriate manner. It is advised that brothers attend meetings on time. Brothers who do not attend lodge at the proper time due to tardiness may find themselves at the end of questions from the
W.M. in the east.

W. M.--Attend to the alarm, Brother Junior, and ascertain the cause.

Junior Deacon opens the door and inquires of the Tyler the cause of the alarm; when the Tyler will report the brethren's names (which we will supposed to be Jones, Brown, and Smith).

J. D. (to the Master) --Brothers Jones, Brown, and Smith are without, and wish admission.

If they are known to the Master, he will say, "Admit them."

[12]*Deacon opens the door, and says, in an under tone of voice, "Come in." These brothers advance to the center of the Lodge, at the altar make the duegard, and sign of the degree on which the Lodge is opened, which is responded to by the Master, and then take their seats among the brethren. No brother is allowed to take his seat until he has saluted the Worshipful Master on entering a Lodge; and if one omits his duty in this respect, he is immediately reminded of it by either the Master or some one of the brethren present. Tyler cautions the brethren, before entering the Lodge, about giving the sign, before passing them through the door; the Junior Deacon the same, as soon as they are in. This officer's station is at the inner door, and it is his duty to address all alarms from the*

---

[12] Here a member errors by giving the duegard and sign that did not represent the degree to which the lodge was opened. This is a mistake that must be prevented as members who are not of a higher degree. It is important for the members to look at the altar and ascertain the degree to which the lodge is opened and present the duegard and sign appropriate for that degree to the W.M.

outside, to report the same to the Master, and get his permission before admitting anyone.

The author remembers seeing the duegard and sign of a Master Mason given, while yet an Entered Apprentice Mason: he was sitting one evening in the Lodge, when a brother of the Third Degree came in, and very carelessly saluted the Master with the Master's duegard and sign, undoubtedly supposing the Lodge open on that degree--a very common error among Masons.

[13]In large cities there are often more than one Lodge. Some cities have ten or twenty, and even more; in the cities of New York and Brooklyn there are one hundred and thirty-five Lodges, besides Chapters, Councils, Commanderies, &c., &c. Consequently, there are Lodge-meetings of some sort of every night in the week, except Sunday, and of course much visiting is going on between the different Lodges. The visitors are not all known to the Masters personally; but the brethren are, generally, acquainted with each other, and of course have often to be vouched for in some of the Lodges, or pass an examination; and for the purpose of giving the reader an idea of the manner in which they are admitted, the author will suppose a case, in order to illustrate it. Jones, Smith, and Brown, belonging to Amity Lodge, No. 323, in Broadway, New York, wish to visit Hiram Lodge, No. 449, of Twenty-fifth Street, and for that purpose go on Lodge night to the hall of Hiram Lodge, No. 449, and ask Tyler for admission. The Tyler will say-- Brothers, are you acquainted with our Master, or any of the brethren in the Lodge? Smith, Jones, and Brown will say,

---

[13] Multiple lodges can meet in one building however each lodge must be chartered independently of the others. Other masonic bodies, Royal Arch, Order of Eastern Star, etc. can meet in the building as well.

yes; or we can't tell, but pass our names in, and if there are any acquainted with us, they will vouch for our masonic standing. The Tyler does so, in the manner already described; and, if they are vouched for by either Master or any brother, they are admitted, the Tyler tells them to what degree the Lodge is open, besides furnishing them with aprons.

On the evening of a Lodge-meeting, brethren get together at an early hour at the Lodge-room, which has been opened and cleaned out by Tyler. On arrival of the Master, and the hour of meeting, the Master repairs to his seat in the east, puts on his hat, sash, yoke, and apron, with gavel in hand, and says: "Brethren will he properly clothed and in order; officers repair to their stations for the purpose of opening."

At this announcement the brethren put on their aprons, and seat themselves around the Lodge-room, while the officers invest themselves with their yokes and aprons, and take their stations as represented in Plate on Page 8., viz.: Senior Warden in the west; Junior Warden in the south; Senior Deacon in front of the Worshipful Master in the east, and a little to his right hand, with a long rod in hand; Junior Deacon at the right hand of the Senior Warden in the west, guarding the inner door of the Lodge, with rod in hand; Secretary at the left of the Worshipful Master, and Treasurer at the right; and, generally, two Stewards on the right and left of the Junior Warden in the south, with rods in hand. After all are thus seated, the Worshipful Master says: "Is Tyler present? If so, let him approach the east."

At this command, Tyler, who is all this time near the outer door of the Lodge, approaches the Worshipful Master's seat in the east, with yoke and apron on.

[14]W. M.--Brother Tyler, your place in the Lodge?

Tyler--Without the inner door.

W. M.--Your duty there?

Tyler--To keep off all cowans and eavesdroppers, and not to pass or repass any but such as are duly qualified and have the Worshipful Master's permission.

W. M.--You will receive the implement of your office (handing him the sword). Repair to your post and be in the active discharge of your duty. (See Note A, Appendix.)

[15]*The Tyler retires to the inside of the outer door of the anteroom, and all Lodge-doors are closed after him.*

W. M. [16](gives one rap with his gavel, Junior Deacon rises up) —Brother Junior Deacon, the first and constant care of Masons when convened?

Junior Deacon--To see that the Lodge is duly tyled.

W. M.--You will address that part of your duty and inform the Tyler that we are about to open a Lodge of Entered

---

[14] The opening of the lodge begins here.
[15] The Tyler secured the door
[16] One wrap of the gavel raises the Wardens

Apprentice Masons (Fellow Crafts, or Master Masons, as the case may be), and direct him to tyle accordingly.

The Deacon opens the door, and says to the Tyler--Brother Tyler, it is the orders of the Worshipful Master that you tyle this Lodge as an Entered Apprentice (Fellow Crafts, or Master Mason, as the case may be); then closes the door, gives one rap (two, if a Fellow Crafts', or three, if a Masters' Lodge), which is responded to by the Tyler.

J. D.--Worshipful Master, the Lodge is titled.

W. M.--How tyled?

J. D.--By a brother of this degree, without the inner door, invested with the proper implement of his office (the sword). W. M.--His duty there?

J. D.--To keep off all cowans and eavesdroppers; suffer none to pass or repass, except such as are duly qualified, and have the Worshipful Master's permission. (Sits down.)

W. M. (one rap, Warden rises to his feet.) --Brother Senior Wardens are you sure that all presents are Entered Apprentice Masons (Fellow Crafts, or Master Masons? as the case may be).

S. W.--I am sure, Worshipful Master, that all presents are Entered Apprentice Masons (or as the case may be).

W. M.--Are you an Entered Apprentice Mason?

S. W.--I am so taken and accepted among all brothers and fellows.

W. M.--Where were you first prepared to be made an Entered Apprentice Mason?

S. W.--In my heart.

W. M.--Where secondly?

S. W.--In a room adjacent to a legally constituted Lodge of such, duly assembled in a place representing the Ground Floor of King Solomon's Temple.

W. M.--What makes you an Entered Apprentice Mason?

S. W.--My obligation.

W. M: How many constitute a Lodge of Entered Apprentice Masons?

S. W.--Seven or more, consisting of the Worshipful Master, Senior and Junior Wardens, Senior and Junior Deacons, Secretary, and Treasurer.

W. M.--The Junior Deacon's place?

S. W.--At the right hand of the Senior Warden in the west.

W. M. ([17]two raps with his gavel, when all the officers of the Lodge rise to their feet.) --Your duty there, brother Junior Deacon?

---

[17] Two raps of all the officers of the lodge is raised.

J. D. (makes the sign of an Entered Apprentice Mason) To carry orders from the Senior Warden in the west to the Junior Warden in the south, and elsewhere around the Lodge, as he may direct, and see that the Lodge is titled.

W. M.--The Senior Deacon's place in the Lodge?

J. D.--At the right hand of the Worshipful Master in the east.

W. M.--Your duty there, brother Senior?

S. D.--To carry orders from the Worshipful Master in the east to the Senior Warden in the west, and elsewhere around the Lodge, as he may direct; to introduce and clothe all visiting brethren; to receive and conduct candidates.

W. M.--The Secretary's place in the Lodge?

S. D.--At the left hand of the Worshipful Master in the east.

W. M.--Your duty, brother Secretary?

Sec.--To observe the Worshipful Master's will and pleasure, record the proceedings of the Lodge, transmit a copy of the same to the Grand Lodge, if required, receive all moneys paid into the Lodge by the hands of the brethren, pass the same over to the Treasurer, and take his receipt for the same.

W. M.--The Treasurer's place in the Lodge?

Sec.--At the right hand of the Worshipful Master in the east.

W. M.--Your duty there, brother Treasurer?

Treas.--To receive all money paid into the Lodge from the hands of the Secretary, keep a regular and just account of the same, and pay it out by the order of the Worshipful Master and the consent of the Lodge.

W. M.--The Junior Warden's station in the Lodge?

Treas.--In the south, Worshipful.

W. M.--Your duty there, brother Junior Warden?

J. W.--As the sun in the south, at high meridian, is the beauty and glory of the day, so stands the Junior Warden in the south, the better to observe the time, call the craft from labor to refreshment superintend them during the hours thereof and see that the means of refreshment be not converted into intemperance or excess; and call them on to labor again, that they may have pleasure and profit thereby.

W. M.--The Senior Warden's station in the Lodge?

J. W.--In the west, Worshipful.

W. M.--Why in the west, brother Senior, and your duty there?

S. W.--To assist the Worshipful Master in opening and closing his Lodge, pay the craft their wages, if any be due, and see that none go away dissatisfied, if in my power to prevent, harmony being the strength of all institutions, more especially of this of ours.

W. M.--The Worshipful Master's station in the Lodge?

S. W.--In the east, Worshipful.

W. M.--Why in the east, and his duty there?

S. W.--As the sun rises in the east, to open and govern the day, so rises the Worshipful Master in the east (here he gives three raps with his gavel, when all the brethren of the Lodge rise, and himself), to open and govern his Lodge, set the craft to work, and give them proper instructions.

W. M.--Brother Senior Warden, it is my orders that this Lodge be opened on the First Degree of Masonry (or second, or Third Degree, as the case may be). For the dispatch of business during which time, all private committees, and other improper, unmasonic conduct, tending to destroy the peace of the same while engaged in the lawful pursuits of Masonry, are strictly forbidden, under no less penalty than a majority of the brethren present, acting under the by-laws of this Lodge, may see fit to inflict: this you will communicate to the Junior Warden in the south, and he to the brethren around the Lodge, that they, having due and timely notice, may govern themselves accordingly.

S. W. (turning to the Junior Warden in the south.) --Brother Junior Warden, you have heard the orders of the Worshipful Master, as communicated to me from the

Worshipful Master in the east. You will take notice and govern yourself accordingly.)

J. W. (to the Lodge.) --Brethren, you have heard the orders of the Worshipful Master, as communicated to me through the Senior Warden in the west. Please take notice and govern yourselves accordingly.

[18]W. M.--Brethren, together on the signs. (The signs of the three degrees are given, if opening on the Third Degree; but if only on the First Degree, Entered Apprentice, the Master would say, together on the sign, and not signs. The Master always leads off in giving the sign or signs. The Master first makes the "duegard" of the First Degree, representing the position of the hands when taking the oath of an Entered Apprentice Mason, which is called the "duegard" of an Entered Apprentice, v "My left hand supporting the Bible, and my right hand resting thereon."

After which the Master makes the sign of an Entered Apprentice Mason, which alludes to the penalty of the Entered Apprentice's obligation, which is imitated by all the brethren present.

[Draw the right hand rapidly across the neck, as represented in the cut, and drop the arm to the side. Remember that the duegard and signs are all made

---

[18] The Master of the lodge is leading the members in giving the signs and duegard of the three degrees of Freemasonry. The signs and duegard are given based upon the degree to which the lodge is opened. Ex. E.A. only the E.A. elements are enacted but the M.M. degree all three are executed.

with right angles, horizontals, and perpendiculars, with very slight, but marked pauses between each motion or part of the sign.]

The Master then makes the duegard of a Fellow Craft, which alludes to the position of the hands when taking the oath of a Fellow Craft Mason.

[The left arm, as far as the elbow, should be held in a horizontal position, and the rest of the arm in a vertical position, forming a square. The right hand detached from the stomach, fingers extending outward.]

After which he gives the sign of a Fellow Craft. which alludes to the penalty of the Fellow Craft obligation.

[In making the duegard and sign of the Fellow Craft, or Second Degree, care must be taken to drop the left arm suddenly and with spirit, as soon as the two motions are accomplished.]

Next is the duegard of a Master Mason, which alludes to the position of the hands when taking the oath of a Master Mason, both hands resting on the Holy Bible, square, and compasses.

And then the sign of a Master Mason, which alludes to the penalty of the obligation of a Master Mason.

[In making this sign, draw the right hand (thumb in) across the stomach as low down as the vest, then drop the hand suddenly.]

The last sign given is the "grand hailing sign of distress."

[Raise the hands as represented in the cut and drop them with spirit. Repeat this three times.]

The words accompanying this sign in the night, or dark, when the sign cannot be seen, are, viz.: "O Lord my God! is there no help for the widow's son?" The Master gives this sign, at the grave of our "Grand Master Hiram Abiff."

Master gives one rap with his gavel; Senior Warden, one; Junior Warden, one. Master one the second time, which is responded to by the wardens a second time, in the west and south, when the master makes the third gavel sound, which is responded to by the Wardens. These three raps are made, when opening the Lodge on the Third Degree; if opening on the Second, two raps only are used; First Degree, one rap each, first given by the Master, then Senior Warden, lastly Junior Warden. After which the Master takes off his hat, and repeats the following passage of Scripture: --

"Behold, how good and how pleasant it is for brethren to dwell together in unity! It is like the precious ointment upon the head, which ran down upon the beard, even Aaron's beard; that went down to the skirts of his garments; as the dew of Hermon, and as the dew that descended upon the mountains of Zion: for there, the Lord commanded the blessing, even life forever more." Amen!

Responded to by all the brethren present: "Amen! So, mote it be!"

W. M.--I now declare this Lodge opened on the First (or, as the case may be) Degree of Masonry. Brother Junior Deacon, you will inform the Tyler. (Deacon opens the Lodge-door and delivers his message to the Tyler.)

W. M.--Brother Senior Deacon, you will attend at the altar. (Here the Senior Deacon steps to the altar, places the square above the compasses, if opened on the First Degree)

COMPASSES, PLACED IN A LODGE OF ENTERED APPRENTICES, "BOTH POINTS COVERED BY THE SQUARE."

W. M. (gives one sound of the gavel.) --All are seated and ready for business

If the Lodge is opened on the Third Degree, and at a regular meeting of the Lodge, the following would be the order of business; but as the reader may be a little anxious, besides curious, about the way and manner of raising the Lodge from the First to the Third Degree, the author will suppose the Lodge open on the First Degree, and, it being a regular Lodge-night, and business to transact, the Lodge must be raised to the Third or Masters' Degree, as no business except that of initiation can be done on the First Degree. The following manner is adopted among Masons at the present day, though there are two or three ways.

W. M. (gives one rap with his gavel.) --Brother Senior Warden, are you sure that all presents are Master Masons? (Or Fellow Crafts, as the case may be.)

S. W.--I am not sure that all present are Master Masons, but will ascertain through my proper officers, and report.

S. W.--Deacons will approach the west (Deacons, both Junior and Senior, repair to the Warden's station in the west); first the Senior Deacon whispers the password of a Master Mason in the ear of the Junior Deacon (Tubal Cain), and the Senior Deacon whispers the same in the Senior Warden's ear, when one Deacon passes up one side of the Lodge, and the other the other side, and, as they go, stop at each brother present for the pass-word, which each brother rises up and whispers in the ear of the Deacon (Tubal Cain); if there are any present that cannot give it, the Deacons pass them by, especially if they are lower degree members (Entered Apprentices or Fellow Crafts), and after the Deacons have gone through the entire Lodge, they meet before the Worshipful Master in the east; the Senior Deacon gets the pass again from the Junior Deacon, and passes it up to the Master, and then they return to the Senior Warden in the west, and pass the same up to him in the same way, and take their seats again, as in . The Warden then rises and says--All present are not Master Masons, Worshipful.

W. M.--All below the degree of Master Mason will please retire while we raise the Lodge. The Junior Deacon says to those below Master Mason, "Brothers, please retire," and he sees that they do so. After they are out, and the door is closed by the Junior Deacon, the Senior Warden says: "All present are Master Masons, Worshipful, and makes the sign of a Master Mason."

W. M.--If you are satisfied that all presents are Master Masons, you will have them come to order as such, reserving yourself for the last.

S. W. (gives three raps with his gavel, when all in the Lodge rise to their feet.)--Brethren, you will come to order as Master Masons.

Brethren all place their hands in the form of a duegard of a Master Mason.

S. W.--In order, Worshipful.

W. M.--Together on the sign, brethren; and makes the sign of a Master Mason (see Figure 6, Page 18.), which is imitated by the officers and brethren, and lastly the Senior Warden. The Master gives one rap, Senior Warden one,

Junior Warden one, and then the Master again one rap, followed up by the Wardens, until they have rapped three times each.

W. M.--I now declare this Lodge open on the Third Degree of Masonry. Brother Junior Deacon inform the Tyler. Brother Senior Deacon address the altar. (Raps once, and the officers and brethren take their seats.)

Order of business as follows,

W. M.--Brother Secretary, you will please read the minutes of our last regular communication.

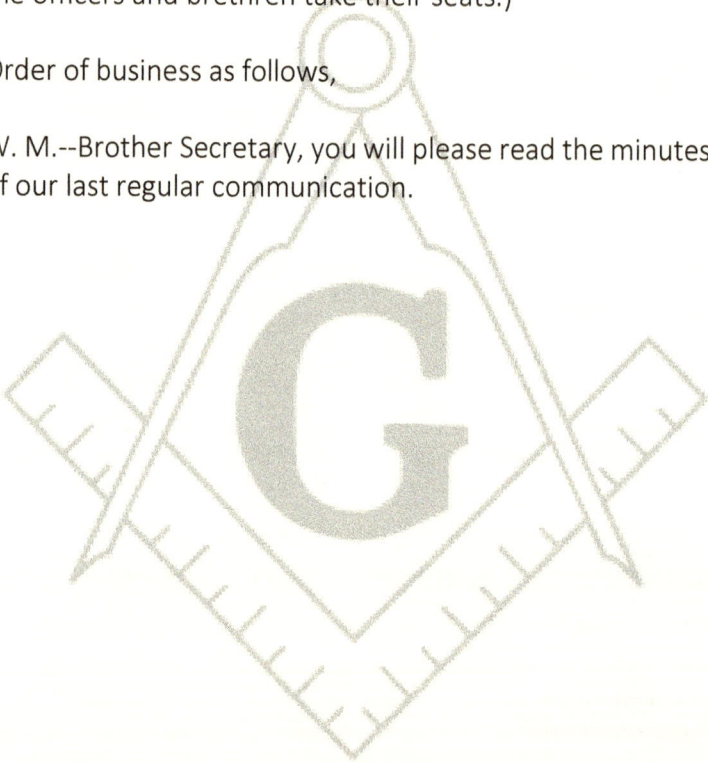

The Secretary reads as follows,

MASONIC HALL, New YORK, December 8, A. L. 5860.

A regular communication of St. John's Lodge, No. 222, of Free and Accepted Masons, was holden at New York, Wednesday, the 10th of November, A. L. 5860.

Present.	Members.
Brother A. B., Worshipful Master.	Brother Luke Cozzans.
" B. C., Senior Warden.	" John Hart.
" C. D., Junior Warden.	" Peter Lewis.
" D. E., Treasurer.	" George Fox.
" E. F., Secretary.	" Robert Onion.
" F. G., Senior Deacon.	" Frank Luckey.
" G. H., Junior Deacon.	" Samuel Slick.
" H. I., Stewards.	" Solomon Wise.
" I. J., "	" Henry Wisdom.
" K. L., Tyler.	" Truman Swift.

VISITING BROTHERS.

Brother James B. Young, of Union Lodge, No. 16, Broadway, New York.

Brother George J. Jones, Rochester Lodge, No. 28, Rochester, New York.

Brother Benjamin Scribble, of Hiram Lodge, No. 37, New Orleans, Louisiana.

Brother Stephen Swift, of Cleveland Lodge, No. 99, Cleveland, Ohio.

Brother Robert Morris, of Lexington Lodge, No. 7, Lexington, Kentucky.

The lodge was opened in due form on the Third Degree of Masonry. The minutes of the last communication of St. John's Lodge were read and confirmed.

The committee on the petition of John B. Crockerberry, a candidate for initiation, reported favorably, whereupon he was balloted for, and duly elected.

The committee on the application of D. C. Woolevert, a candidate for initiation, reported favorably; whereupon he was balloted for, and the box appearing foul, he was declared rejected.

The committee on the application of William S. Anderson, a candidate for initiation, having reported unfavorably, he was declared rejected, without a ballot.

A petition for initiation from Robert Chase, of Jersey City, accompanied by the usual fee of ten dollars ($10), and recommended by Brothers Hart, Lewis, and Onion, was referred to a committee of investigation, consisting of Brothers Slick, Wise, and Swift.

Brother Samuel Brevoort, an Entered Apprentice, having applied for advancement, was duly elected to the Second Degree; and Brother Thomas Jansen, a Fellow Craft, was, on his application for advancement, duly elected to the Third Degree in Masonry.

The Lodge of Master Masons was then closed, and a Lodge of Entered Apprentices opened in due form.

Mr. Charles Fronde, a candidate for initiation, being in waiting, was duly prepared, brought forward, and initiated as an Entered Apprentice Mason in due and ancient form, he is paying the further sum of five dollars ($5).

Lodge of Entered Apprentices closed, and a Lodge of Fellow Crafts opened in due form.

Brother Stephen Currie, an Entered Apprentice, being in waiting, was duly prepared, brought forward, and passed to the degree of a Fellow Craft, he is paying the further sum of five dollars ($5).

The Lodge of Fellow Crafts closed, and a Lodge of Master Masons opened in due form.

Brother John Smith, a Fellow Craft, being in waiting, was duly prepared, brought forward, and raised to the sublime degree of a Master Mason, he is paying the further sum of five dollars ($5).

Amount received this evening, as follows: --

Petition of Robert Chase	$10.00
Fellow Craft Charles Fronde	5.00
Fellow Craft Stephen Currie	5.00
Master Mason John Smith	<u>5.00</u>
	$25.00

All of which was paid over to the Treasurer.

There being no further business, the Lodge was closed in due form and harmony.

SAMUEL SLICK, Secretary.

Approved:

SOLOMON NORTHUS, W. M.

Such is the form which has been adopted as the most convenient mode of recording the transactions of a Lodge at the present day.

The minutes of a Lodge should be read at the close of each meeting, that the brethren may suggest any necessary alterations or additions, and then at the beginning of the next regular meeting, that they may be confirmed.

W. M.--Brother Senior Warden, have you any alterations to propose?

S. W. (makes the sign of a Master Mason, see Fig. 6, p 18.) --I have none, Worshipful.

W. M.--Have you any, Brother Junior Warden?

J. W. --None, Worshipful.

W. M.--Has any brother around the Lodge any alterations to propose? (None offering) W. M.--Then, brethren, the motion is on the confirmation of the minutes of our last communication; all that are in favor of their confirmation will make it known by the usual sign of a Mason those opposed, by the same sign, which is called the usual sign of a Mason. The question of confirmation is simply a question whether the secretary has faithfully and correctly recorded the transactions of the Lodge.

If it can be satisfactorily shown by any brother that there are any omissions or mis entries, this is the time to correct them.

SECOND ORDER OF BUSINESS

W. M. (reading and referring petitions.) --If the secretary has any petitions on his table, he will report to the Lodge, as follows: Worshipful Master, there are two petitions for membership, which are as follows.

FORM OF PETITION.

To the Worshipful Master, Wardens, and Brethren of St. John's Lodge, No. 222, of Free and Accepted Masons:

The petition of the subscriber respectfully shows, that, entertaining a favorable opinion of your ancient institution, he is desirous of being admitted a member thereof, if found worthy. His place of residence is New York City, his age thirty-eight years, his occupation a bookseller. (Signed) ABNER CRUFF.

Recommended by Brothers Jones, Carson, and Fox.

NEW YORK, December 1, 1860.

Sec.--The next petition is from Peter Locke, recommended by Brothers Derby and Jackson. Both these petitions are accompanied by the usual fee of ten dollars each.

W. NI. --Brethren, what is your pleasure respecting these petitions of Gruff and Locke?

Brother Hand--I would move that they be received, and a committee of investigation be appointed.

Brother Fast--I second that motion, Worshipful.

W. M.--Brethren, you have heard the motion. All those in favor of the motion, make it known by the usual sign; all to the contrary, the same.

W. M.--The petitions are received, and I would appoint, on the application of Mr. Cruff, Brothers Brevoort, Gore, and Acker-man; and, on the petition of Mr. Locke, Brothers Derby, Hart, and Barnes.

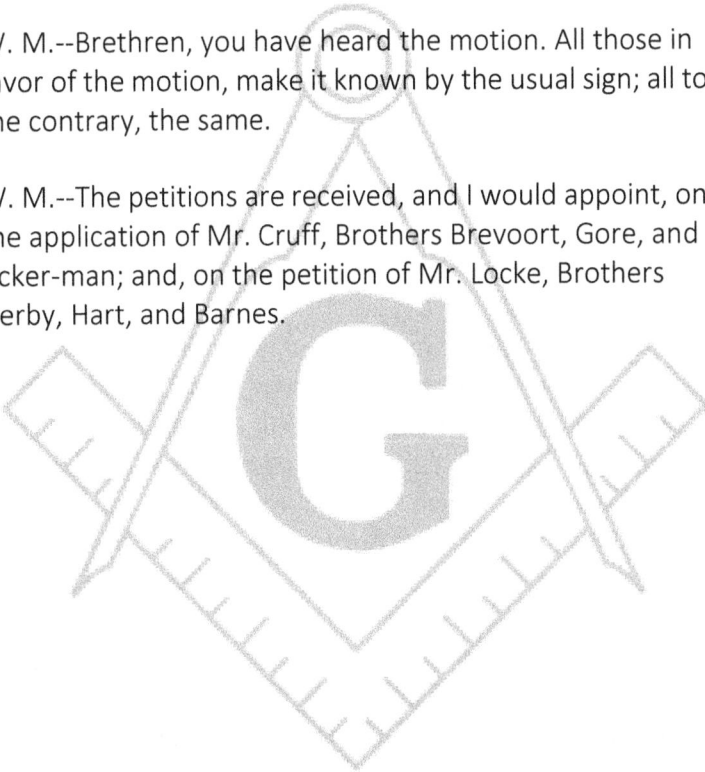

THIRD ORDER OF BUSINESS

W. M. (receiving reports of committees.) --Brother Secretary, are there any committee reports due on your desk?

Sec.--There are two reports, Worshipful. One on the application of Mr. Robert Granger, and one on the application of Mr. Brady.

W. AL--Are the chairmen of those committees' present?

Brother Pepper--Worshipful, as chairman of the committee to whom was referred the application of Mr. Robert Granger, I would say to the Lodge that I have examined into his character and find it good, and, consequently, report on it favorably. I think he will make a good Mason. In his younger days, he was wild; but now he is considered very steady, and a good member of society. (Here, sometimes, great, and lengthy discussion arises. Some very conscientious and discreet brother thinks a more thorough inquiry should have been made respecting Mr. Robert Granger's early history, the result of which is that he is not balloted for until the next regular meeting. This is no common thing, though.)

W. M.--Is the chairman of the committee to whom was referred the application of Peter Locke present?

Brother Melville--Worshipful, I am chairman of that committee, and report favorably. He is recommended as one of the best of men.

W. M.--Brethren, what is your pleasure with the petition of Mr. Locke?

Brother Jones--I move, Worshipful, that the report be received, committee discharged, and the candidate balloted for. Brother Jackson--I second that motion.

W. M.--Brethren, you have heard the motion. All in favor of it, make it known by the usual sign; the contrary, the same.

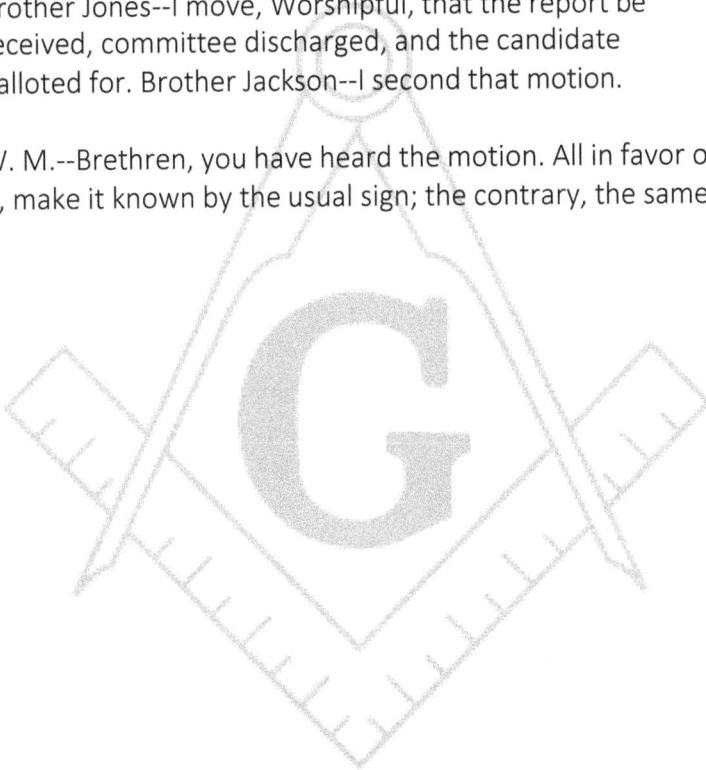

FOURTH ORDER OF BUSINESS

W. M. (balloting for candidates, or admission.) --Brother Secretary, are there any candidates to be balloted for?

Sec.--There are, Worshipful, two, viz.: Joseph Locker and Reuben Bruce.

W. M.--Brethren, we are about to ballot for two applicants for the First Degree in Masonry. The first is the petition of Mr. Joseph Locker. Anything for or against this gentleman is now in order. (Here, if any brother has anything for or for Mr. Locker, he is privileged to speak on the subject.) If nothing is offered, the Master says:

W. M.--If there is nothing to offer, we will proceed to ballot. Brother Senior Deacon, you will prepare the ballot-box.

Senior Deacon takes the ballot-box (which is a small box, five or six inches square, with two drawers in it, and a small hopper in the top, a hole from which passes down into the first drawer, which is empty and shoved in, while the lower one is drawn out and nearly full of both black and white balls), places the box on the altar in the middle of the Lodge, and takes his seat again.

W. M.--Brethren, you will proceed to ballot.

The balloting is done as follows, viz.: Master first; Secretary calls the names, commencing with the Senior Warden down to the Tyler, and, as their names are called, each Mason steps up to the box at the altar, makes the sign of Master Mason to the Master, and then takes from the lower drawer of the ballot-box a ball (white or black, as he sees fit), deposits it in the hopper above, and retires to his seat. So, all votes.

W M.--Have all voted? If so, Brother Senior Deacon, you will close the ballot.

Senior Deacon closes the drawer, and carries the box to the Junior Warden in the south He nulls out the top drawer, looks to see if the drawer is "clear" or not, and then closes it and hands it to the Deacon, who carries it to the Senior Warden in the west for his examination. As the Deacon leaves the Junior Warden's station, the Master says to him:

W. M.--Brother Junior Warden, how stands the ballot in the south?

J. W. (makes the sign of a Master Mason, see Figure 6, page 18.) --Clear in the south, Worshipful. (If not clear, and there should be a black ball or two, he would say--Not clear in the south, Worshipful.)

By this time, the Senior Warden has examined, and the Master inquires of him:

W. M.--Brother Senior Warden, how stands the ballot in the west?

S. W.--Clear (or not) in the west, Worshipful. (Making the sign.)

By this time, the Deacon has arrived at the Worshipful Master's station in the east. He looks in the box, and says:

W. M.--And clear (or not clear) in the east. Brethren, you have elected (or not) Mr. Joseph Locker to the First Degree in Masonry.

The other candidate is balloted for in the same manner.

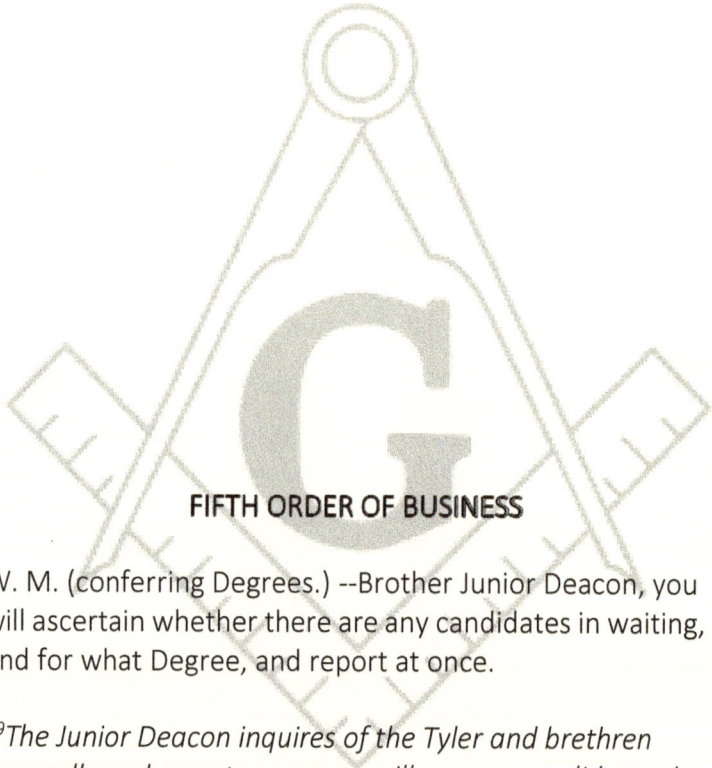

FIFTH ORDER OF BUSINESS

W. M. (conferring Degrees.) --Brother Junior Deacon, you will ascertain whether there are any candidates in waiting, and for what Degree, and report at once.

[19]*The Junior Deacon inquires of the Tyler and brethren generally and reports someone will name a candidate who has been previously balloted for, who will be waiting in the anteroom.*

---

[19] The candidate begins the process of initiation here. The J.D. is responsible for candidates and accompany them on their masonic journey throughout the ritual. An E.A. Degree will be conferred upon the candidate at this point.

J. D.--There is one, or two (as easy may be) now in waiting for the First Degree, Mr. Candidate and Mr. John Milke.

W. M.--Brethren, there seems to be a good deal of business on hand this evening; but my business engagements are such as to render it impossible for me to be present late, consequently we will confer the Degree upon Mr. Candidate only, and will call a special communication next week to attend to Mr. Milke's wants. You will inform Mr. Milke, Brother Junior Deacon, of our decision, and not keep him any longer waiting. You will also say to Mr. Candidate, that as soon as we finish the regular business of the Lodge, he can have the First Degree conferred on him.

Junior Deacon does his duty.

SIXTH ORDER OF BUSINESS

W. M. No unfinished business.

SEVENTH ORDER OF BUSINESS

W. M. Brethren, if there is no further business before this Lodge of Master Masons, we will proceed to close the same, and open an Entered Apprentices' Lodge, for the purpose of initiation.

Here Lodges differ, in the mode of lowering from a Masters to an Entered Apprentices' Lodge. Some close entirely, and open on the First; but we will adopt a short way, that Lodges have at the present day.[20]

---

[20] Here the E.A. lodge is closed, and the M.M. lodge is open.

W. M.--Brother Senior Warden, are you sure all presents are Entered Apprentice Masons?

S. W.--I am sure, Worshipful, all presents are Entered Apprentice Masons.

W. M.--If you are sure all present are Entered Apprentice Masons, you will have them come to order as such, reserving yourself for the last.

S. W. Brethren, you will come to order as Entered Apprentice Masons.

The members place their hands in the position of a duegard of an Entered Apprentice. When the Master makes "the sign, by drawing his hand across his throat, all follow suit; Worshipful then makes one rap with the gavel, Senior Warden one, and the Junior Warden one.[21]

W. M.--I now declare this Lodge of Master Masons closed, and an Entered Apprentice in its stead. Brother Junior Deacon inform the Tyler; Brother Senior Deacon, attend at the altar (which is placing both points of the compasses under the square). (The worshipful Master gives one rap, which seats the whole Lodge.) Brother Junior Deacon, you will take with you the necessary assistants (the two Stewards), repair to the anteroom, where there is a candidate in waiting (Mr. Candidate, for the First Degree in Masonry), and, when duly prepared, you will make it known by the usual sign (one rap).

_____

[21] The lodge is closed

[22]*The Junior Deacon and his assistants retire to the anteroom, but before they leave the Lodge-room they step to the altar and make the sign of the First Degree to the Master. It is the duty of the Secretary to go out into the anteroom with them, and before the candidate is required to strip, the Secretary gets his assent to the following interrogations.*

[23]Sec: Do you seriously declare, upon your honor, that, unbiassed by friends, and uninfluenced by mercenary motives, you freely and voluntarily offer yourself a candidate for the mysteries of Masonry?

Candidate: Yes (or I do).

Sec. Do you seriously declare, upon your honor, that you are prompted to solicit the privileges of Masonry by a favorable opinion of the institution, a desire for knowledge, and a sincere wish of being serviceable to your fellow-creatures?

Candidate: Yes.

Sec. Do you seriously declare, upon your honor, that you will con-form to all the ancient established usages of the Order?

Candidate: Yes.

---

[22] The J.D. and secretary leaves the lodge to engage the candidate. The secretary interrogates the candidate.
[23] Interrogation

The Secretary returns to the Lodge, and reports that the candidate has given his assent to the interrogations.

The candidate is now requested to strip.

[24]J. D. Mr. Candidate, you will take off your coat, shoes, and stockings, also your vest and cravat; and now your pantaloons; here is a pair of drawers for you. You will now slip your left arm out of your shirtsleeve, and put it through the bosom of your shirt, so that your arm and breast may be naked. The Deacon now ties a handkerchief or hoodwink over his eyes, places a slipper on his right foot, and afterwards puts a rope, called a cable-two, once round his neck, letting it drag behind.

The figure is a representation of the candidate duly and truly prepared for the First Degree in Masonry.

[25]*The Junior Deacon now takes the candidate by the arm and leads him forward to the door of the Lodge, and gives three distinct knocks, when the Senior Deacon. on the inside, rises to his feet, makes the sign of an Entered Apprentice to the Master, and says:*

S. D.--Worshipful Master, there is an alarm at the inner door of our Lodge. W. M.--You will address the alarm and ascertain the cause. (The Deacon repairs the door, gives three distinct knocks, and then opens it.)

S. D.--Who comes here?

---

[24] Candidate is stripped and dressed according to masonic law prior to initiation.
[25] The candidate is led into the lodge by his companion J.D.

[26]J. D. Mr. Candidate, who has long been in darkness, and now seeks to be brought to light, and to receive a part in the rights and benefits of this worshipful Lodge, erected to God, and dedicated to the holy Sts. John, as all brothers and fellows have cloned before.

S. D.--Mr. Candidate, is it of your own free-will and accord?

Mr. Candidate.--It is.

S. D.--Brother Junior Deacon, is he worthy, and qualified?

J. D.--He is.

S. D.--Duly and truly prepared?

J. D.--He is.

S. D.--Of lawful age, and properly vouched for?

J. D.--He is.

S. D.--By what further right or benefit does he expect to gain admission?

J. D.--By being a man, free born, of good repute, and well recommended.

S. D.--Is he such?

J. D.--He is.

---

[26] The J.D. makes the responses for the candidate

S. D.--Since he is in possession of all these necessary qualifications, you will wait with patience until the Worshipful Master is informed of his request, and his answer returned.

Deacon closes the door and repairs to the altar before the Worshipful Master, raps once on the floor with his rod, which is responded to by the Master with his gavel, when the same thing is passed through with as at the door, and the Master says:

W. M.--Let him enter and be received in due form.

The Senior Deacon takes the compasses from off the altar, repairs to the door, opens it, and says:

S. D.--Let him enter and be received in due form.

Senior Deacon steps back, while the Junior Deacon, with candidate, enters the Lodge, followed by the two Stewards. As they advance, they are stopped by the Senior Deacon, who presents one point of the compasses to the candidate's naked left breast, and says:

[27]S. D. Mr. Candidate, on entering this Lodge for the first time, I receive you on the point of a sharp instrument pressing your naked left breast, which is to teach you, as it is a torture to your flesh, so should the recollection of it

---

[27] This is performed to impress upon the candidate the importance of the great undertaking he has agreed upon.

ever be to your mind and conscience, should you attempt to reveal the secrets of Masonry unlawfully.

The Junior Deacon now leaves the candidate in the hands of the Senior Deacon and takes his seat at the right hand of the Senior Warden in the west; while the Senior Deacon, followed by the two Stewards, proceeds to travel once regularly around the Lodge-room, as follows. Senior Deacon takes the candidate by the right arm, advances a step or two, when the Master gives one rap with his gavel.

W. M.--Let no one enter on so important a duty without first invoking the blessing of the Deity. Brother Senior Deacon, you will conduct the candidate to the center of the Lodge and cause him to kneel for the benefit of prayer.

S. D.--Mr. Candidate, you will kneel.

Worshipful Master now leaves his seat in the east, approaches candidate, kneels by his side, and repeats the following prayer.[28]

[29]W. M.--Vouchsafe Thine aid, Almighty Father of the Universe, to this our present convention; and grant that this candidate for Masonry may dedicate and devote his life to Thy service and become a true and faithful brother among us! Endue him with a competency of Thy divine wisdom, that, by the secrets of our art, he may be better

---

[28] W.M. assist the candidate at this point

[29] The Worshipful Master prays for the candidate in that he receives wisdom to inculcate the principle of Freemasonry in the honor of the Almighties name. This is to imbue the candidate with wisdom.

enabled to display the beauties of brotherly love, relief, and truth, to the honor of Thy Holy Name. Amen.

Responded to by all, "So mote it be."

W. M. (rising to his feet, taking candidate by the right hand, placing his left on his head.) Mr. "Candidate" in whom do you put your trust?

[30]Candidate: **In God!**

W. M.--Since in God you put your trust; your faith is well founded. Arise follow your [31]Deacon and fear no danger.

[32]*The Master retires to his seat in the east, and while the Deacon (S. D.) is attending the candidate once around the Lodge-room, he repeats the following passage: --*

"[33]Behold, how good and how pleasant it is for brethren to dwell together in unity!"

The reading is so timed as to be concluded when they have passed once around the Lodge-room to the Junior Warden's station in the south; as they pass each. officer's station, east, south, and west, they give one sound with their gavels, viz.: first the Master, one (•): J. W., one (•); S. W., one (•); which has a good effect on the candidate, the sounds being

---

[30] Here the candidate is prompted by the J.D. to answer in God. Though prompted the candidate can feel to whom he places his trust and answers with vigor and humility.

[31] The Deacon is the J.D. here the candidate learns to meaning of brotherly love as he rises and fears no danger.

[32] The W.M. reads the passage from the Bible

[33] This is an excerpt from Psalms 133. It presses upon the candidate's conscience the importance of brotherly love, charity, and truth.

near his ears as he passes by (his Deacon passing close up). Having passed once around the Lodge, they halt at the Junior Warden's station in the south.

[34]J. W. Who comes here?

Deacon (S. D.) --Mr. Candidate. who has long been in darkness, and now seeks to be brought to light, and to receive a part in the rights and benefits of this Worshipful Lodge, erected to God, and dedicated to the holy St. John, as all brothers and fellows have done before.

J. W.--Mr. Candidate, is it of your own free will and accord?

Mr. Candidate--It is.

J. W.--Brother Senior Deacon, is he worthy and qualified? S. D.--He is.

J. W.--Duly and truly prepared? S. D.--He is.

J. W.--Of lawful age, and properly vouched for?

S. D.--He is.

J. W.--By what further right or benefit does he expect to gain admission?

---

[34] Candidate arrives here from the S.W. station in the West to be questioned as before.

S. D.--By being a man, free born, of good repute, and well recommended.

J. W.--Since he is in possession of all these necessary qualifications, I will suffer him to pass on to the Senior Warden's station in the west.

Senior Warden, disposing of him in the same manner as the Junior Warden, suffers him to pass on to the Worshipful Master in the east, who makes the same inquiries as did the Wardens in the south and west, after which the Master says:

W. M.--From whence come you, and whither are you traveling?

S. D.--From the west and traveling toward the east.

W. M.--Why leave you the west and travel toward the east?

S. D.--In search of light.

[35]W. M.--Since light is the object of your search, you will reconduct the candidate, and place him in charge of the Senior Warden in the west, with my orders that he teach this candidate to approach the east, the place of light, by advancing with one upright, regular step to the first stop, the heel of his right placed in the hollow of his left foot, his body erect at the altar before the Worshipful Master in the east.

---

[35] The candidate seeks that which is upright which is light (understanding, knowledge, and Wisdom)

Senior Deacon conducts candidate back to the Senior Warden in the west, and says:

S. D.--Brother Senior Warden, it is the orders of the Worshipful Master, that you teach this candidate to approach the east, the place of light, by advancing on one regular upright step to the first stop; the heel of his right foot in the hollow of his left (see Fig. 14, Page 93), his body erect at the altar before the Worshipful Master in the east.

Senior Warden leaves his seat, comes down to the candidate, faces him towards the Worshipful Master, and requests him to step off with his left foot, bringing the heel of his right in the hollow of his left before the candidate is requested to do this, he is led by the Warden within one pace of the altar). Senior Warden reports to the Worshipful Master.

S. W.--The candidate is in order and awaits your further will and pleasure.

The Master now leaves his seat in the east, and, approaching the candidate, says:

W. M.--Mr. Candidate, before you can be permitted to advance any farther in Masonry, it becomes my duty to inform you, that you must take upon yourself a solemn oath or obligation, appertaining to this degree, which I, as Master of this Lodge, assure you will not materially interfere with the duty that you owe to your God, yourself, family, country, or neighbor. Are you willing to take such an oath?

Candidate--I am.

W. M.--Brother Senior Warden, you will place the candidate in due form, which is by kneeling on his naked left knee, his right forming the angle of a square, his left hand supporting the Holy Bible, square, and compasses, his right hand resting thereon.

The Warden now places, or causes the candidate to be placed, in the position commanded by the Worshipful Master.

W. M.--Mr. Candidate, you are now in position for taking upon

"Kneeling on my naked left knee, my right forming a square; my left supporting the Holy Bible, square, and compasses, my right resting thereon[36]

yourself the solemn oath of an Entered Apprentice Mason, and, if you have no objections still, you will say I, and repeat your name after me.

---

[36] Candidate kneels

Master gives one rap with his gavel which is the signal for all present to assemble around the altar.

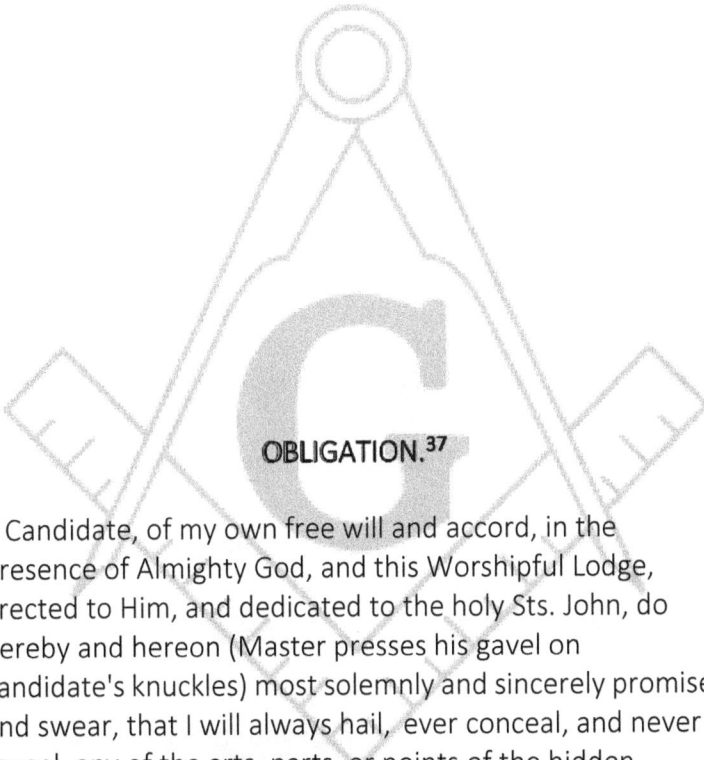

OBLIGATION.[37]

I, Candidate, of my own free will and accord, in the presence of Almighty God, and this Worshipful Lodge, erected to Him, and dedicated to the holy Sts. John, do hereby and hereon (Master presses his gavel on candidate's knuckles) most solemnly and sincerely promise and swear, that I will always hail, ever conceal, and never reveal, any of the arts, parts, or points of the hidden mysteries of Ancient Free Masonry, which may have been, or hereafter shall be, at this time, or any future period, communicated to me, as such, to any person or persons whomsoever, except it be to a true and lawful brother Mason, or in a regularly constituted Lodge of Masons; nor

---

[37] The candidate takes the obligation. As stated above "what makes you a mason - may obligation." The obligation is what makes the candidate a mason not the ritual alone.

unto him or them until, by strict trial, due examination, or lawful information, I shall have found him, or them, as lawfully entitled to the same as I am myself. I furthermore promise and swear that I will not print, paint, stamp, stain, cut, carve, mark, or engrave them, or cause the same to be done, on anything movable or immovable, capable of receiving the least impression of a word, syllable, letter, or character, whereby the same may become legible or intelligible to any person under the canopy of heaven, and the secrets of Masonry thereby unlawfully obtained through my unworthiness.

All this I most solemnly, sincerely promise and swear, with a firm and steadfast resolution to perform the same, without any mental reservation or secret evasion of mind whatever, binding myself under no less penalty than that of having my throat cut across, my tongue torn out by its roots, and my body buried in the rough sands of the sea, at low-water mark, where the tide ebbs and flows twice in twenty-four hours, should I ever knowingly violate this my Entered Apprentice obligation. So, help me God, and keep me steadfast in the due performance of the same.

W. M.--In token of your sincerity, you will now detach your hands, and kiss the book on which your hands rest, which is the Holy Bible.

After the candidate has kissed the Bible, the Master asks him:

W. M.--In your present condition, what do you most desire?

Candidate --Light.

W. M.--Brethren, you will stretch forth your hands, and assist me in bringing our newly made brother to light.

[38]*Here the brethren surrounding the altar place their hands in form of duegard of an Entered Apprenticed Mason.*

[39]W. M.--"In the beginning God created the heavens and the earth. And the earth was without form, and void; and darkness was upon the face of the waters. And God said, let there be light, and there was light."

Worshipful Master now gives one rap which is the signal for all to be seated but himself, he is remaining at the altar. I should remark here, that at the word "light," the Deacon strips off the hoodwink from the candidate's eyes but keeps him yet kneeling at the altar.

W. M.--Brother Senior Deacon, I will now thank you to remove the cable-tow. (Rope is taken off candidate's neck.)

Some Masters say--As we now hold the brother by a stronger tie.

W. M.--My brother, on being brought to light in this degree, you discover both points of the compasses hid by the square, which is to signify that you are yet in darkness as respects Masonry, you have only received the degree of an Entered Apprentice. You also discover the three great

---

[38] The brothers make the duegard and sign of the E.A. while the candidate is blind folded.
[39] The brothers here make stamps on the floor to create drama. The candidate can appreciate this experience,

lights of Masonry, with the help of the three lesser. The three great lights in Masonry are the Holy Bible, square, and compasses, which are thus explained: the Holy Bible is the rule and guide of our faith and practice; the square, to square our actions; the compasses, to circumscribe and keep us within bounds with all mankind, but more especially with a brother Mason. The three lesser lights are the three burning tapers which you see placed in a triangular form about this altar. They represent the sun, moon, and Master of the Lodge; and as the sun rules the day, and the moon governs the night, so ought the Worshipful Master to endeavor to rule and govern his Lodge, with equal regularity.

[40]W. M. You next discover me as the Master of this Lodge, approaching you from the east, under the duegard, sign, and step of an Entered Apprentice Mason which is the token of my brotherly love and favor, present you my right hand and with it the grip and word of an Entered Apprentice. Grip me, brother, as I grip you. As you are yet uninformed, your Deacon will answer for you. (Senior Deacon.)

W. M. (looking the Deacon in the eye, while holding candidate by the right hand.) --I hail.

S. D.--I conceal.

---

[40] The Master grips the candidate with the right hand and instructs him on what to do.

W. M.--What do you conceal?

S. D.--All the secrets of Masons, in Masons, to which this token alludes.

W. M.--What is that?

S. D.--A grip.

W. M.--Of what?

S. D.--Of an Entered Apprentice Mason.

W. M.--Has it a name?

S. D.--It has.

W. M.--Will you give it me?

S. D.--I did not so receive it; neither can I so impart it.

W. M.--How will you dispose of it?

S. D.--I will letter it or halve it.

W. M.--Letter it and begin.

S. D.--No, you begin.

W. M.--Begin you.

S. D.--A.

W. M.--B.

S. D.--O.

W. M.--Z.

S. D.--Bo.

W. M.--Az.

S. D. Says Boaz.

W. M. Rise, my brother, and salute the Junior and Senior Wardens as an obligated Entered Apprentice.

Here Lodges differ; some only pass candidate once around the room, and, as he passes the officers' stations, he gives the duegard and sign of an Entered Apprentice; while other Lodges require him to halt at the Wardens' stations, and pass through with the following ceremony, viz.: The Deacon takes candidate by the right arm, and passes around the altar to the Junior Warden's station in the south, stops, gives one rap with his rod on the floor, which is responded to by the Junior Warden with his gavel, once.

J. W.--Who comes here?

S. D.--An obligated Entered Apprentice.

J. W.--How shall I know him to be such?

S. D.--By signs and tokens.

J. W--What are signs?

S. D.--Right angles, horizontals, and perpendiculars (⌐, =
, ‖).

J. W.--What are tokens?

S. D.--Certain friendly or brotherly grips, by which one Mason may know another, in the dark as well as in the light,

J. W.--Give me a sign.

Senior Deacon gives the duegard and directs the candidate to do likewise.

J. W.--What is that?

S. D.--A duegard.

J. W.--Has it an allusion?

S. D.--It has; it alludes to the manner in which my hands were placed when I took upon myself the obligation of an Entered Apprentice Mason.

J. W.--Have you any further signs?

S. D.--I have. (Makes the sign of an Entered Apprentice. See Fig 2, p. 17)

J W.--What is that?

S. D.--Sign of an Entered Apprentice Mason.

J. W.--Has it an allusion?

S. D.--It has, to the penalty of my obligation.

J. W.--Have you any further sign?

S. D.--I have not; but I have a token.

J. W.--Advance your token.

Senior Deacon makes candidate take the Junior Warden by the right hand.

J. W.--I hail.

S. D.--I conceal.

J. W.--What do you conceal?

S. D.--All the secrets of Masons, in Masons, to which this (here presses his thumbnail on the joint) token alludes.

J. W.--What is that?

S. D.--A grip.

J. W--Of what?

S. D.- Of an Entered Apprentice Mason.

J. W.--Has it a name?

S. D.--It has.

J. W.--Will you give it to me?

S. D.--I did not so receive it, neither will I so impart it.

J. W.--How will you dispose of it?

S. D.--I will letter it, or halve it,

J. W.--Letter it and begin.

S. D.--No, you begin.

J. W.--Begin you.

S. D.--A.

J. W.--B.

S. D--O.

J. W.--Z.

S. D.--Bo.

J. W-Az.

S. D. Says Boaz

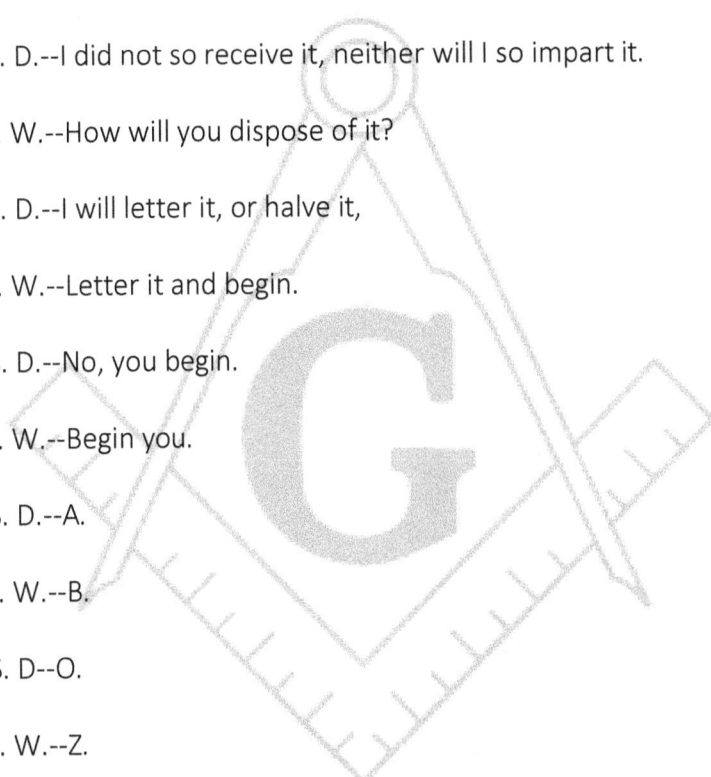

J. W.--I am satisfied and will suffer you to pass on to the Senior Warden in the west for his examination.

The Deacon and candidate pass on to the Senior Warden's station, where the same ceremony is gone through with, and suffers them to pass on to the Worshipful Master in the east. As they leave the west and are to the Master station in the east, he gives one rap with his gavel, when they halt. The Master takes a white linen apron (sometimes a lambskin, which is kept for such purposes), approaches the candidate, hands it to him rolled up, and says:

W. M.--Brother, I now present you with a lambskin or white apron, which is an emblem of innocence and the badge of a Mason, more ancient than the Golden Fleece or Roman Eagle, and, when worthily worn, more honorable than the Star and Garter, or any other order that can be conferred on you at this time, or any future period, by kings, princes, and potentates, or any other persons, except it be by Masons. I trust that you will wear it with equal pleasure to yourself and honor to the fraternity. You will carry it to the Senior Warden in the west, who will teach you how to wear it as an Entered Apprentice.

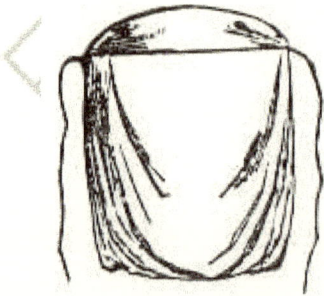

ENTERED APPRENTICE'S APRON.

Deacon conducts candidate back to the west, and says:

S. D.--Brother Senior Warden, it is the order of the Worshipful Master, that you teach this new-made brother how to wear his apron as an Entered Apprentice.

The Senior Warden takes the apron and ties it on the candidate, with the flap turned up, remarking to the candidate as he does so: This is the way, Candidate, which Entered Apprentices wore their aprons at the building of King Solomon's Temple, and so you will wear yours until further advanced. Senior Deacon now reconducts the candidate to the Worshipful Master in the east.

W. M.--Candidate, agreeably to an ancient custom, adopted among Masons, it is necessary that you should be requested to deposit something of a metallic kind or nature, not for its intrinsic valuation, but that it may be laid up among the relics in the archives of this Lodge, as a memento that you were herein made a Mason. Anything, brother that you may have about you, of a metallic nature, will be thankfully received--a button, pin, five or ten cent piece--anything, my brother.

Candidate feels for something--becomes quite confused. On examination, or reflection, finds himself very destitute, not being able to contribute one pin, his Deacon having been careful to take everything from him, in the ante-room, before he entered the Lodge;--finally stammers out that he has nothing of the kind with him, but if permitted to pass out into the ante-room, where his clothes are, he will contribute. This the Master refuses to do, of course, which only helps confuse the candidate increasingly. After the Master has kept the candidate in this suspense some moments, he says:

[41]W. M.--Candidate, you are indeed an object of charity-- almost naked, not one cent, no, not even a button or pin to bestow on this Lodge. Let this ever have, my brother, a lasting effect on your mind and conscience; and remember, should you ever see a friend, but more especially a brother, in a like destitute condition, you will contribute as liberally to his support and relief as his necessities may seem to demand and your ability permit, without any material injury to yourself or family.

W. M.--Brother Senior Deacon, you will now reconduct this candidate to the place from whence he came and reinvest him with that which he has been divested of and return him to the Lodge for further instruction.

Senior Deacon takes candidate by the arm, leads him to the center of the Lodge, at the altar before the Worshipful Master in the east, makes duegard and sign of an Entered Apprentice, and then retires to the anteroom.

After the candidate is clothed, the deacon ties on his apron, and, returning to the Lodge, conducts him to the Worshipful Master in the east, who orders the Deacon to place him in the northeast corner of the Lodge, which is at the Master's right.

---

[41] This is to press upon the candidate that all men are equal and when found in a destitute state we can rely on our brother and humanity to provide a means of substance.

W. M.--Candidate, you now stand in the northeast corner of this Lodge, as the youngest Entered Apprentice, an upright man and Mason, and I give it to you strictly in charge as such ever to walk and act. (Some Masters preach great sermons to candidates on this occasion.) Brother, as you are clothed as an Entered Apprentice, it is necessary you should have the working-tools of an Entered Apprentice, which are the twenty-four-inch gauge and common gavel.

W. M.--The twenty-four-inch gauge is an instrument made use of by operative masons to measure and lay out their work; but we, as Free and Accepted Masons, are taught to make use of it for the more noble and glorious purpose of dividing our time. It being divided into twenty-four equal parts, is emblematical of the twenty-four hours of the day which we are taught to divide

42

into three parts, whereby we find a portion for the service of God and the relief of a distressed worthy brother, a portion for our usual avocations, and a portion for refreshment and sleep.

---

42 Divide the day into three equal parts. This is symbolic but practical as well.

W. M.--The common gavel is an instrument made use of by operative masons to break off the superfluous corners of rough stones, the better to fit them

for the builder's use.
but we, as Free and
Accepted Masons, are
taught to make use of it

43

for the more noble and glorious purpose of divesting us minds and consciences of all the vices and superfluities of life, thereby fitting us, as living stones, for that spiritual building, that house not made with hands, eternal in the heavens.

W. M.--Candidate, there is a lecture to this Degree, consisting of three sections, which you will at your earliest opportunity commit to memory. The first section treats of the manner of your initiation; the second section, the reasons wily, &c.; the third section, the form, furniture, lights, &c., &c. This lecture commences as follows:

---

[43] Gavel is the remove unwanted negative behavior from one's life thereby making the heart, mind, and body and fit vessel for work in this life and the world to come.

FIRST SECTION.

Q. From whence came you? (Some say, As an Entered Apprentice Mason.)

A. From a Lodge of the Sts. John of Jerusalem.

Q. What came you here to do?

A. To learn to subdue my passions and improve myself in Masonry.

Q. Then I presume you are a Mason?

A. I am so taken and accepted among all brothers and fellows.

Q. How do you know yourself to be a Mason?

A. By having been often tried, never denied, and willing to be tried again.

Q. How shall I know you to be a Mason?

A. By certain signs, a token, a word, and the perfect points of my entrance.

Q. What are signs?

A. Right angles, horizontals, and perpendiculars (⌐, =, ‖).

Q. What are tokens?

A. Certain friendly or brotherly grips, by which one Mason may know another in the dark as well as in the light. Q. Give me a sign.

Here is the sign of Entered Apprentice. (See Fig. 2, p. 17)

Q. Has that an allusion?

A. It has; to the penalty of my obligation.

Q. Give me a token.

Here is the sign of Entered Apprentice. (See Fig. 2, p. 17)

Q. I hail.

A. I conceal.

Q. What do you conceal?

A. All the secrets of Masons, in Masons, to which this (here press with thumbnail the first joint hard) token alludes.

Q. What is that?

A. A grip.

Q. Of what?

A. Of an Entered Apprentice Mason.

Q. Has it a name?

A. It has.

Q. Will you give it me?

A. I did not so receive it, neither will I so impart it.

Q. How will you dispose of it?

A. I will letter it or halve it.

Q. Letter it and begin.

A. No, you begin.

Q. Begin you. (Some say, no, you begin.)

A. A.

Q. B.

A. O.

Q. Z.

A. Bo.

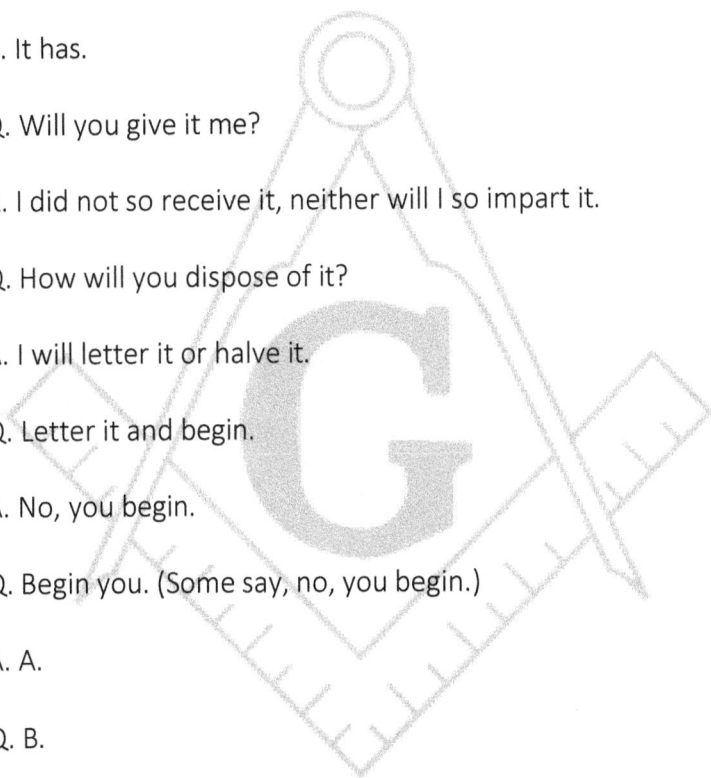

Q. Az.

A. Boaz.

Q. Where were you first prepared to be made a Mason?

A. In my heart.

Q. Where were you next prepared?

A. In a room adjacent to a regularly constituted Lodge of Free and Accepted Masons.

Q. How were you prepared?

A. By being divested of all metals, neither naked nor clothed; barefoot nor shod, hoodwinked, with a cable-tow around my neck; in which condition I was conducted to the door of a Lodge by a friend, whom I afterward found to be a brother.

Q. How did you know it to be a door, being hoodwinked?

A. By first meeting with resistance, afterward gaining admission.

Q. How gained you admission?

A. By three distinct knocks.

Q. What were said to you from within?

A. Who comes here?

Q. Your answer?

A. Mr. ------ , who has long been in darkness, and now seeks to be brought to light, and to receive a part in the rights and benefits of this worshipful Lodge, erected to God, and dedicated to the holy Ste. John, as all brothers and fellows have done before.

Q. What were you then asked?

A. If it was of my own free will and accord; if I was worthy and qualified; duly and truly prepared; of lawful age and properly vouched for. All of which being answered in the affirmative, I was asked by what further right or benefit I expected to gain admission.

Q. Your answer?

A. By being a man, free born, of good repute, and well recommended.

Q. What followed?

A. I was directed to wait with patience until the Worshipful Master should be informed of my request, and his answer returned.

Q. What answer did he return?

A. Let him enter and be received in due form.

Q. How were you received?

A. On the point of a sharp instrument pressing my naked left breast.

Q. How were you then disposed of?

A. I was conducted to the center of the Lodge, caused to kneel, and attend prayer.

Q. After attending at prayer, what were you then asked?

A. In whom I put my trust.

Q. Your answer?

A. In God.

Q. What followed?

A. My trust being in God, I was taken by the right hand, and informed that my faith was well founded; ordered to arise, follow my Deacon, and fear no danger.

Q. Where did you follow your Deacon?

A. Once around the Lodge, to the Junior Warden's station in the south, where the same questions and like answers were asked and returned as at the door.

Q. How did the Junior Warden dispose of you?

A. He bid me be conducted to the Senior Warden in the west, and he to the Worshipful Master in the east, were

The same questions were asked and like answers returned as before.

Q. How did the Worshipful Master dispose of you?

A. He ordered me to be reconducted to the Senior Warden in the west, who taught me to approach the east by one upright, regular step, my feet forming an angle of an oblong square, my body erect, at the altar before the Worshipful Master in the east.

Q. What did the Worshipful Master then do with you?

A. He made me a Mason in due form.

Q. What was that due form?

A. Kneeling on my naked left knee, my right forming a square, my left hand supporting the Holy Bible, square, and compasses, my right resting thereon, in which due form I took the solemn oath of an Entered Apprentice, which is as follows:

Q. After the obligation, what were you then asked?

A. What I most desired.

Q. Your answer?

A. Light.

Q. Did you receive light?

A. I did, by the order of the Worshipful Master and the assistance of the brethren.

Q. On being brought to light, what did you first discover?

A. The three great lights in Masonry, with the help of the three lesser.

Q. What are the three great lights in Masonry?

A. The Holy Bible, square, and compasses.

Q. What are their Masonic use?

[44]A. The Holy Bible is the rule and guide to our faith and practice; the square, to square our actions; and the compasses, to [45]circumscribe and keep us within bounds with all mankind, but more especially with a brother Mason.

Q. What are the three lesser lights?

A. Three burning tapers, in a triangular position.

Q. What do they represent?

A. The sun, moon, and Master of the Lodge.

---

[44] Symbolic of the Holy Bible explained

[45] Circumscribe means to restrict. As mason we evaluate ourselves again the moral principles that are demonstrated through the Holy Bible. See Leviticus 19. Love you neighbor as yourself is the mantra found through the Bible. We not only align ourselves with our brothers' needs but also humanity, mason and nonmason alike.

Q. Why so?

A. Because, as the sun rules the day, and the moon governs the night, so ought the Worshipful Master to endeavor to rule and govern his Lodge, with equal regularity.

Q. What did you then discover?

A. The Worshipful Master approaching me from the east, under the duegard and sign of an Entered Apprentice; who, in token of his brotherly love and favor, presented me with his right hand, and with it the grip and word of an Entered Apprentice and ordered me to arise and salute the Junior and Senior Wardens as an Entered Apprentice.

Q. After saluting the Wardens, what did you then discover?

[46]A. The Worshipful Master approaching me from the east a second time, who presented me with a lambskin or white linen apron which he informed me was an emblem of innocence and the badge of a Mason; that it had been worn by kings, princes, and potentates of the earth; that it was more ancient than the Golden Fleece or Roman Eagle; more honorable than the Star or Garter, or any other order that could be conferred on me at that or any time thereafter by king, prince, potentate, or any other person, except he be a Mason; and hoped that I would wear it with equal Praise to myself and honor to the fraternity; and ordered me to carry it to the Senior Warden in the west, who taught me how to wear it as an Entered Apprentice.

---

[46] The apron explained

Q. How should an Entered Apprentice wear his apron?

A. With the flap turned up.

Q. After being taught to wear your apron as an Entered Apprentice, what were you then informed?

A. That, agreeably to an ancient custom, adopted in every regulated and well-governed Lodge it was necessary that I should be requested to deposit something of a metallic kind, not from its intrinsic valuation, but that it might be laid up, among the relics in the archives of the Lodge, as a memorial that I was therein made a Mason; but, on strict examination, I found myself entirely destitute.

Q. How were you then disposed of?

A. I was ordered to be returned to the place from whence I came, and reinvested of what I had been divested of, and returned to the Lodge for further instructions.

Q. On your return to the Lodge, where were you placed, as the youngest Entered Apprentice?

A. In the northeast corner, my feet forming a right angle, my body erect, at the right hand of the Worshipful Master in the east, an upright man and Mason, and it was given me strictly in charge ever to walk and function as such.

Q. What did the Worshipful Master then present you with?

A. The working-tools of an Entered Apprentice Mason, which are the twenty-four-inch gauge and common gavel.

Q. What is their use?

[47]A. The twenty-four-inch gauge is an instrument made use of by operative masons, to measure and lay out their work; but we, as Free and Accepted Masons, are taught to make use of it for the more noble and glorious purpose of dividing our time. It being divided into twenty-four equal parts is emblematical of the twenty-four hours of the day, which we are taught to divide into three parts, whereby we find a portion for the service of God and the relief of a distressed worthy brother, a portion for our usual avocations, and a portion for refreshment and sleep.

The [48]common gavel is an instrument made use of by operative masons, to break off the superfluous corners of rough stones, the better to fit them for the builder's use; but we, as Free and Accepted Masons, are taught to make use of it for the more noble and glorious purpose of divesting our minds and consciences of all the vices and superfluities of life, thereby fitting us, as living stones of that spiritual building, that house not made with hands, eternal in the heavens.

This ends the first section of the lecture as given in Lodges at the present day; but as some Lodges persist still in keeping up the old lecture as revealed by William Morgan, in1826, and by Bernard, Allyn, Richardson, and

---

[47] Twenty-four-inch gauge explained. This tools will assist the candidate with making good use of the time in which you are given.
[48] The common gavel is the tool by which the mason removes the negative from his life thereby resulting in an improved version of himself if which does not happen without study.

others, the author will give it, that it may go to the world a complete Masonic lecture.

Q. What were you next presented with?

A. A new name.

Q. What was that?

A. Caution.

Q. What does it teach?

A. It teaches me, as I was barely instructed in the rudiments of Masonry, that I should be cautious over all my words and actions, especially when before its enemies.

Q. What were you next presented with?

A. Three precious jewels.

Q. What were they?

A. A listening ear, a silent tongue, and a faithful heart.

Q. What do they teach?

[49]A. A listening ear teaches me to listen to the instructions of the Worshipful Master, but more especially to the cries of a worthy distressed brother. A silent tongue teaches me to be silent in the Lodge, that the peace and harmony thereof may not be disturbed, but more especially before

---

[49] The trust of a candidate and the obligation that he has sworn to be impressed upon him here.

the enemies of Masonry. A faithful heart, that I should be faithful and keep and conceal the secrets of Masonry and those of a brother when delivered to me in charge as such, that they may remain as secure and inviolable in my breast as in his own, before being communicated to me.

Q. What were you next presented with?

A. The Grand Master's check-word.

Q. What was that?

A. Truth.

Q. How explained?

A. Truth is a divine attribute, and the foundation of every virtue. To be good and true are the first lessons we are taught in Masonry. On this theme we contemplate, and by its dictates endeavor to regulate our conduct; hence while influenced by this principle, hypocrisy and deceit are unknown among us, sincerity and plain dealing distinguish us, and the heart and tongue join in promoting each other's welfare and rejoicing in each other's prosperity.

With a few other interrogations and answers the old lecture ends. These interrogations and answers are embodied in the new-fangled lecture as already given; they relate only to the demand for something of a metallic kind, reinvestment of candidate's clothing, northeast corner of the Lodge..

SECOND SECTION.

Q. Why were you divested of all metals when made a Mason?

A. For the reason, first, that I should carry nothing offensive or defensive into the Lodge; second, at the building of King Solomon's Temple, there was not heard the sound of an axe, hammer, or any tool of iron.

Q. How could a building of that stupendous magnitude be erected without the aid of some iron tool?

A. Because the stones were hewed, squared, and numbered at the quarries where they were raised; the trees felled and prepared in the forests of Lebanon, carried by sea in floats to Joppa, and from thence by land to Jerusalem, where they were set up with wooden mauls, prepared for that purpose; and, when the building was completed, its several parts fitted with such exact nicety, that it had more the resemblance of the handy workmanship of the Supreme Architect of the universe than of that of human hands.

Q. Why were you neither naked nor clothed?

A. Because Masonry regards no one for his worldly wealth or honors; it is the internal, and not the external qualifications of a man that should recommend him to be made a Mason.

Q. Why were you neither barefoot nor shod?

A. It was in conformity to an ancient Israelitish custom: we read in the book of Ruth, that it was their manner of changing and redeeming; and to confirm all things, a

Mason plucked off his shoe and gave it to his neighbor, and that was testimony in Israel. This then we do in confirmation of a token, and as a pledge of our fidelity; thereby signifying that we will renounce our own will in all things and become obedient to the laws of our ancient institution.

Q. Why were you hoodwinked, and a cable-tow put about your neck?

A. For the reason, first, as I was then in darkness, so I should keep the whole world in darkness as far as it related to the secrets of Free-Masonry. Secondly: in case I had not submitted

to the manner and mode of my initiation, that I might have been led out of the Lodge, without seeing the form and beauty thereof.

Q. Why were you caused to give three distinct knocks?

A. To alarm the Lodge and inform the Worshipful Master that I was prepared for Masonry, and, in accordance to our ancient custom, that I should ask. "Ask, and ye shall receive; seek, and ye shall find; knock, and it shall be opened unto you."

Q. How did you apply this to your situation in Masonry?

A. I asked the recommendation of a friend to become a Mason; through his recommendation I sought admission; I knocked at the door of the Lodge and it was opened unto me.

Q. Why were you received on the point of a sharp instrument pressing your naked left breast?

A. As that was an instrument of torture to my flesh, so might the recollection of it be to my conscience, should I ever presume to reveal the secrets of Free-Masonry.

Q. Why were you caused to kneel and attend prayer?

A. Because no man should ever enter upon a great and important undertaking without first imploring the blessings of Deity.

Q. Why were you asked in whom you put your trust?

A. Because, agreeably to our most ancient institution, no Atheist could be made a Mason; it was therefore necessary that I should put my trust in Deity, or no oath would have been considered binding among Masons.

Q. Why were you taken by the right hand, ordered to arise, follow your Deacon, and fear no danger?

A. It was to assure me, as I could not foresee nor avoid danger, that I was in the hands of a true and trusty friend, in whose fidelity I might with safety confide.

Q. Why were you conducted once around the Lodge?

A. That the brethren might see that I was duly and truly prepared.

Q. Why were you caused to meet with the several obstructions in your passage?

A. Because there were guards placed at the south, west, and east gates of the courts of King Solomon's Temple, to see that none passed or repassed but such as were duly and truly prepared and had permission; it was therefore necessary that I should meet with these several obstructions, that I might be duly examined before I could be made a Mason.

Q. Why were you caused to kneel on your naked left knee?

A. Because the left side is considered to be the weakest part of man; it was therefore to show that it was the weaker part of Masonry I was then entering upon, being that of an Entered Apprentice.

Q. Why were you caused to rest your right hand on the Holy Bible, square, and compasses?

A. Because the right hand was supposed by our ancient brethren to be the seat of fidelity, and so they worshipped Deity under the name of Fides, which was supposed to be represented by the right hands joined, and by two human figures holding each other by the right hand; the right hand, therefore, we masonically use to signify in the strongest manner possible the sincerity of our intentions in the business in which we are engaged.

Q. Why were you presented with a lambskin or white linen apron, which is the badge of a Mason?

A. Because the lamb, in all ages, has been deemed an emblem of innocence; he, therefore, who wears the lambskin as a badge of a Mason is thereby continually reminded of that purity of life and conduct which is essentially necessary to his gaining admission into that celestial Lodge above, where the Supreme Architect of the universe presides.

Q. Why were you requested to deposit something of a metallic kind?

A. To remind me of my extremely poor and penniless state, and that, should I ever meet with a friend, more especially with a brother, in like destitute circumstances, I should contribute as liberally to his relief as his circumstances demanded, without any material injury to myself.

Q. Why were you conducted to the northeast corner of the Lodge, as the youngest Entered Apprentice, and there caused to stand upright like a man, your feet forming a square--receiving at the same time a solemn charge ever to walk and act uprightly before God and man?

A. Because the first stone of a building is usually laid in the northeast corner. I was therefore placed there to receive my first instructions on where to build my future Masonic and moral edifice.

THIRD SECTION.

Q. What is a Lodge?

A. [50]A certain number of Masons duly assembled, with the Holy Bible, square, and compasses, and charter, or warrant empowering them to work.

Q. Where did our ancient brethren usually meet?

A. On a high hill or in a low valley.

Q. Why so?

A. The better to observe the approach of cowans, or eavesdroppers, ascending or descending.

Q. What is the form and covering of a Lodge?

A. An oblong square, extending from east to west, between the north and south, from the earth to the heavens, and from the surface to the center.

Q. Why of such vast dimension?

A. To signify the universality of Masonry, and that a Mason's charity should be equally extensive.

Q. What supports this vast fabric?

A. Three great pillars, constituting Wisdom, Strength, and Beauty.

---

[50] A proper lodge must have the items listed herein.

Q. Why are they so called?

A. Because it is necessary there should be wisdom to contrive, strength to support, and beauty to adorn all great and important undertakings.

Q. By whom are they represented?

A. By the Worshipful Master, and the Senior and Junior Wardens.

Q. Why are they said to represent them?

A. The Worshipful Master represents the pillar of Wisdom because he should have wisdom to open his Lodge, set the craft at work, and give them proper instructions. The Senior Warden represents the pillar of Strength, it being his duty to assist the Worshipful Master in opening and closing his Lodge, to pay the craft their wages, if any be due, and see that none go away dissatisfied, harmony being the strength of all institutions, more especially of ours. The Junior Warden represents the pillar of Beauty, it being his duty at all times to observe the sun at high meridian, which is the glory and beauty of the day.

Q. What covering has a Lodge?

A. A clouded canopy, or starry-decked heavens, where all good Masons hope to arrive, &c., &c. (See Masonic Monitor.)

Q. What furniture does a Lodge have?

A. The Holy Bible, square, and compasses.

Q. To whom are they dedicated?

A. The Bible is dedicated to God, the square to the Master, and the compasses to the craft.

Q. Why are they thus dedicated?

A. The Bible is dedicated to God, because it is the inestimable gift of God to man.

Q. What are the ornaments of a Lodge?

A. The mosaic pavement, the indented tessel, and the blazing star.

Q. What are they?

A. The mosaic pavement is a representation of the Ground Floor of King Solomon's Temple, with a blazing star in the center; the indented tessel, that beautiful tessellated border which surrounds it.

Q. Of what are they emblematical?

A. The mosaic pavement represents this world, which, though checkered over with good and evil, yet brethren may walk to-ether thereon, and not stumble.
(See Monitor.)

Q. How many lights does a Lodge have?

A. Three.

Q. How are they situated?

A. East, west, and south.

Q. None in the north?

A. No.

Q. Why none in the north?

A. Because this and every other Lodge is, or ought to be, a true representation of King Solomon's Temple, which was situated north of the ecliptic; the sun and moon, therefore, darting their rays from the south, no light was to be expected from the north. We, therefore, masonically, term in the north a place of darkness.

Q. How many jewels does a Lodge have?

A. Six: three movable, and three immovables.

Q. What are movable jewels?

A. The rough ashler, the perfect ashler, and the trestle-board.

Q. What are they?

A. Rough ashler is a stone in its rough and natural state; the perfect ashler is also a stone, made ready by the working-tools of the fellow craft, to be adjusted in the building; and the trestle-board is for the master workman to draw his plans and designs upon.

Q. What do they remind us of?

A. By the rough ashler we are reminded of our rude and imperfect state by nature; by the perfect ashler of that state of perfection at which we hope to arrive by a virtuous education, our own endeavors, and the blessing of God; and by the trestle-board we are also reminded that, as the operative workman erects his temporal building agreeably to the rules and designs laid down by the Master on his trestle-board, so should we, both operative and speculative, endeavor to erect our spiritual building agreeably to the rules and designs laid down by the Supreme Architect of the universe, in the great book of Revelation, which is our spiritual, moral, and Masonic trestle-board.

Q. What are the three immovable jewels?

A. The square, level, and plumb.

Q. What do they masonically teach us?

A. The square teaches morality; the level, equality: and the plumb teaches rectitude of life.

Q. How should a Lodge be situated?

A. Due east and west.

Q. Why so?

A. Because, after Moses had safely conducted the children of Israel through the Red Sea, by Divine command he erected a tabernacle to God, and placed it due east and west, which was to commemorate to the latest posterity that miraculous east wind that wrought their mighty deliverance--this was an exact model of Solomon's Temple; since which time every well-regulated and governed Lodge is, or ought to be, so situated.

Q. To whom were Lodges dedicated in ancient times?

A. To King Solomon.

Q. Why so?

A. Because it was said he was our most ancient Grand Master, or the founder of our present system.

Q. To whom in modern times?

A. To St. John the Baptist and St. John the Evangelist, who were two eminent Christian patrons of Masonry; and since their time there is, or ought to be, represented in every

regular and well-governed Lodge a certain "point within a circle," the point representing an individual brother, the circle the boundary-line of his conduct beyond which he is never to suffer his prejudices or passions to betray him. This circle is embodied by two perpendicular parallel lines,

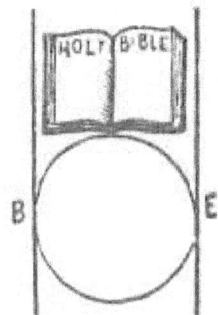

representing St. John the Baptist and St. John the Evangelist; and upon the top rest the Holy Scriptures. In going around this circle, we necessarily touch upon these two lines, as well upon the Holy Scriptures, and while a Mason keeps himself circumscribed within their precepts it is impossible that he should materially err.

This ends the lecture on the Entered Apprentices' Degree. But very few Masons are sufficiently posted in these lectures to answer every inquiry respecting then. Not one in a hundred ever gets them perfect, none but a few aspiring members seeking after office take the trouble to commit them to memory, and some of these do so very imperfectly. Most Masters, at the present day, qualify themselves for the office of Master by purchasing Richardson's or Avery Allyn's Masonic exposures. These works have, of course, to be amended. On perusing the present work the reader will be surprised at the striking resemblance it bears to the works just mentioned, especially in the lectures; but let him mark the alterations, principally at the commencement of each lecture

In some Lodges the following lecture is used, especially in the Northwestern States:

Q. What are the points of your profession?

A. Brotherly love, relief, and truth.

Q. Why so?

Q. Brother. You informed me that I should know you by certain signs, and tokens, and words, and the points of your entrance. You have already satisfied me as to the signs and words. I now require you to explain to me the points of your entrance: how many, and what are they?

A. They are four: The Guttural, the Pectoral, the Manual, and the Pedestal, which allude to the four cardinal virtues, viz.; Temperance, Fortitude, Prudence, and Justice.

[51]**Temperance** is that due restraint upon our affections and passions which renders the body tame and governable and frees the mind from the allurements of vice. This virtue should be the constant practice of every Mason, as he is thereby taught to avoid excess, or contracting any licentious or vicious habit, the indulgence of which might lead him to disclose some of those valuable secrets which he has promised to conceal and never reveal, and which would consequently subject him to the contempt and detestation of all good Masons. See "Guttural," This virtue alludes to the Mason's obligation, which is the Guttural.

Fortitude is that noble and steady purpose of the mind, whereby we are enabled to undergo any pain, peril, or danger, when prudentially deemed expedient. This virtue is equally distant from rashness and cowardice; and, like the former, should he deeply impressed upon the mind of every Mason, as a safeguard or security against any illegal attack that may be made, by force or otherwise, to extort from him any of those secrets with which he has been so solemnly entrusted; and which virtue was emblematically represented upon his first admission into the Lodge, on the

---

[51] The nature of a mason must be governed by the four virtues herein explained. The candidate must learn and understand how to apply the virtue's and thereby be a representative of the order and the Almighty

point of a sharp instrument pressing his naked left breast. This alludes to the Pectoral.

Prudence teaches us to regulate our lives and actions agreeably to the dictates of our reason, and is that habit by which we wisely judge, and prudentially determine, on all things relative to our present, as well as to our future happiness. This virtue should be the invariable practice of every Mason never to for the government of his conduct while in the Lodge, but also when abroad in the world. It should be particularly addressed in all strange and mixed companies, never to let fall the least sign, token, or word, whereby the secrets of Masonry might be unlawfully obtained. Especially, brother in Masonry, you should always remember your oath as an Entered Apprentice, while kneeling at the altar, on your naked left knee, your left hand supporting the Holy Bible, square, and compasses, your right resting thereon, which alludes to the Manual.

Justice is that standard or boundary of right which enables us to render to every man without distinction his just due. This virtue is not only consistent with Divine and human laws but is the very cement and support of civil society; and as Justice in. a great measure constitutes the good man, so should it be the invariable practice of every Mason never to deviate from the minutest principles thereof.

The charge you received while standing in the northeast corner of the Lodge, your feet forming a right angle, was an allusion to the Pedestal.

Q. How did Entered Apprentices serve their Master in ancient times, and how should they in modern times?

A. With freedom, fervency, and zeal.

Q How were they represented?

A. [52]By Chalk, Charcoal, and Clay.

Q. Why were they told to represent them?

A. Because it was said there was nothing freer than chalk, which, under the slightest touch, leaves a trace behind; nothing more fervent than charcoal to melt--when well lit, the most obdurate metals will yield; nothing more zealous than clay, or our mother earth, to bring forth.

CHARGE AT INITIATION INTO THE FIRST DEGREE

[53]BROTHER: As you are now introduced into the first principles of Masonry, I congratulate you on being accepted into this ancient and honorable order; ancient, as having existed from time immemorial; and honorable, as tending in every particular so to render all men who will conform to its precepts. No human institution was ever raised on a better principle, or more solid foundation; nor were ever more excellent rules and useful maxims laid down than are inculcated in the several Masonic lectures The greatest and best of men in all ages have been encouragers and promoters of the art, and have never

---

[52] The W.M. is the chief office of the lodge. He must be revered not out of fear but love of the order and guidance of his leadership. The Worshipful Master represents Wisdom and must be addressed in this manner. It is the elevation of his peers that selected him based upon his qualities to lead with love and wisdom.

[53] The Candidate is not an E.A. mason and is charged by the W.M. to inculcate the manners of a mason.

deemed it derogatory to their dignity to level themselves with the fraternity, extend their privileges, and patronize their assemblies.

There are three great duties, which, as a Mason, you are strictly to observe and inculcate--to God, your neighbor, and yourself. To God, in never mentioning His name but with that reverential awe which is due from a creature to his Creator; to implore His aid in all your laudable undertakings, and to esteem Him as your chief good. To your neighbor, in acting upon the square, and doing unto him as you would he should do unto you: and to yourself, in avoiding all irregularity and intemperance, which may impair your facilities or debase the dignity of your profession. A zealous attachment to these duties will ensure public and private esteem.

In the State you are to be a quiet and peaceable citizen, true to your government, and just to your country; you are not to countenance disloyalty or rebellion, but patiently submit to legal authority, and conform with cheerfulness to the government of the country in which you live.

In your outward demeanor be particularly careful to avoid censure or reproach. Let not interest, favor, or prejudice bias your integrity, or influence you to be guilty of a dishonorable action. And although your frequent appearance at our regular meetings is earnestly solicited, yet it is not meant that Masonry should interfere with your necessary avocations, for these are on no account to be neglected; neither are you to suffer your zeal for the institution to lead you into arguments with those who, through ignorance, may ridicule it. But, at your leisure hours, that you may improve in Masonic knowledge, you

Always converse with well-informed brethren, who will be always as ready to give as you will be ready to receive instruction.

Finally, keep sacred and inviolable the mysteries of the Order, as these are to distinguish you from the rest of the community, and mark your consequence among Masons. If, in the circle of your acquaintance, you find a person desirous of being initiated into Masonry, be particularly careful not to recommend him, unless you are convinced he will conform to our rules; that the honor, glory, and reputation of the institution may be firmly established, and the world at large convinced of its good effects.

[54]You, brother, are a preacher of that religion, of which the distinguishing characteristics are universal benevolence and unbounded charity. You cannot, therefore, but be fond of the Order, and zealous for the interests of Freemasonry, which, in the strongest manner, inculcates the same charity and benevolence, and which, like that religion, encourages every moral and social virtue, which introduces peace and good-will among man. kind, and is the center of union to those who otherwise might have remained at a perpetual distance. So that whoever is warmed with the spirit of Christianity, must esteem, must love Freemasonry. Such is the nature of our institution, that, in all our Lodges, union is cemented by sincere attachment, hypocrisy and deceit are unknown, and pleasure is reciprocally communicated by the cheerful observance of every obliging office. Virtue, the

---

[54] This charge is given for spiritual leaders of religion no matter the belief system.

grand object in view, luminous as the meridian sun, shines refulgent on the mind, enlivens the heart, and converts cool approbation into warm sympathy and cordial affection.

Though every man, who carefully listens to the dictates of reason, may arrive at a clear persuasion of the beauty and necessity of virtue, both public and private. Yet it is a full recommendation of a society to have these pursuits continually in view, as the sole objects of their association; and these are the laudable bonds which unite us in one indissoluble fraternity.

PERFECT ASHLER 55

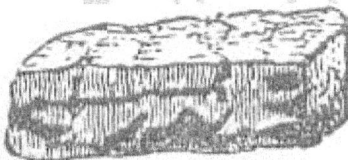

ROUGH ASHLER 56

[57]FELLOW CRAFT OR SECOND DEGREE

---

[55] The state that we strive to become. A stone shaped for the use of the GAOTU. We have raised our minds to higher states of consciousness and our attributes demonstrate we are in a better state.

[56] The state that we find ourselves before the removing of our rough edges. The lower passions are prevalent at this stage

[57] Ceremonies have been omitted and the candidate is now preparing for F.C degree. We start with the question of the F.C.

W. M.--Brother Junior Deacon, you will take with you the necessary assistance and repair to the anteroom, where there is a candidate in waiting for the second degree in Masonry; and when you have him prepared, make it known by the usual sign.

The Junior Deacon, with the two Stewards accompanying him, steps to the center of the Lodge, makes the duegard and sign of a Fellow Craft, and passes out of the Lodge into the anteroom.

J. D.--Well, Candidate, you will have to be prepared for this Degree as all have been before you. You, of course, can have no serious objection?

Candidate. --I have not.

J. D.--Then you will take off your boots, coat, pants, vest-necktie, and collar; and here is a pair of drawers, unless you have a pair of your own. Now you will slip your right arm out of your shirtsleeve, and put it through the bosom of your shirt, that your right arm and breast may he naked.

[58]*The Deacon here ties a hoodwink, or handkerchief, over both eyes. (In the time of Morgan, it was the usage to cover only one eye.) The Junior Deacon then ties a rope, by Masons called a cable-tow, twice around his arm. (Formerly, the rope was put twice round the candidate's neck.) Some Lodges follow the old custom now, but this is a rare thing. The reader will, however, do well to recollect these hints, as they are particular points.*

The right foot and knee of the candidate are made bare by rolling up the drawers, and a slipper should be put on his left foot. This being accomplished, the candidate is duly and truly prepared. (See engraving.)

---

[58] The candidate is prepared for the F.C. degree as in the E.A. The manner of dress differs from the E.A.

The Deacon now takes the candidate by the arm, and leads him forward to the door of the Lodge; and upon arriving there he gives three raps, when the Senior Deacon, who has taken his station on the inside door of the Lodge, reports to the Master as follows:

S. D.--Worshipful Master (making the sign of a Fellow Craft), there is an alarm at the inner door of our Lodge.

W. M.--You will address the alarm and ascertain the cause.

The Deacon gives three raps, which are responded to by the Junior Deacon, and answered to by one rap from the Senior Deacon inside, who opens the door, and says:

S. D.--Who comes here?

J. D. (Deacon.) --Candidate, who has been regularly initiated as Entered Apprentice, and now wishes to receive more light in Masonry by being passed to the degree of Fellow Craft.

S. D. (turning to candidate.) --Candidate, is it of your own free-will and accord?

Candidate--It is.

S. D.--Brother Junior Deacon, is he duly and truly prepared, worthy, and qualified?

J. D.--He is.

S. D.--Has he made suitable proficiency in the preceding degree?

J. D.--He has.

S. D.--And properly vouched for?

J. D.--He is.

S. D.--Who vouches for him?

J. D--A brother.

S. D.--By what further right, or benefit, does he expect to gain admission?

J. D.--By the benefit of a pass.

S. D.--Has he that pass?

J. D.--He has it not, but I have it for him.

S. D.--Advance and give me the pass. (Some say, advance the pass.)

Junior Deacon whispers in the Senior Deacon's ear the password, "Shibboleth."

S. D.--The pass is right. You will wait with patience until the Worshipful Master is informed of your request, and his answer returned.

The Senior Deacon then closes the door, and repairs to the center of the Lodge, before the Worshipful Master in the east, and sounds his rod twice on the floor, which is responded to by the Master with his gavel, when the same interrogations and answers are repeated by the Master and Deacon as at the door. The Master then says:

W. M--Let him enter, in the name of the Lord, and be received in due form.

The Senior Deacon then takes the square from the altar, and, repairing to the door, he opens it, and says:

S. D.--Let him enter in the name of the Lord and be received in due form.

The Junior Deacon advances through the door, followed by the two Stewards, when the Senior Deacon stops them by placing the angle of the square against the candidate's right breast.

S. D. (pressing square against candidate's breast.)-- Candidate, on entering this Lodge the first time you were received on the points of the compass: I now receive you on the angle of the square, which is to teach you that the square of virtue should be the rule and guide of your conscience in all future transactions with mankind.

The Senior Deacon now takes the candidate by the right arm, followed by the Stewards, and conducts him twice around the Lodge, counting from the Junior Warden's station in the south, during which time the Master reads the following passage of Scripture:

[59]"Thus, he showed me: and behold, the Lord stood upon a wall made by a plumbline, with a plumbline in his hand. And the Lord said unto me, Amos, what seest thou? And I said, A plumbline. Then said the Lord, Behold, I will set a plumbline in the midst of my people Israel; I will not again pass by them anymore."--Amos vii. 7, 8.

While going around the Lodge, as the Deacon and candidate pass the officers' stations in the south, west, and east, they (the officers) sound the gavel as follows: the first time going round, one rap each; the second time, two raps each. By the time the Master has finished reading the above passage of Scripture, the candidate and Deacon have passed around the room twice and arrived at the Junior Warden's station in the south.

J. W. (giving two raps, which are responded to by the deacon.) --Who comes here?

S. D. (Deacon.) --Candidate, who has been regularly initiated Apprentice, and now wishes to receive more light in Masonry, by being passed to the Degree of Fellow Craft.

J. W. (turning to candidate.) --Candidate, is it of your own free-will and accord?

Candidate--It is.

J. W.-Brother Senior Deacon, is he duly and truly prepared, worthy, and qualified?

S D.--He is.

---

[59] The book of Amos is referenced here.

J. W.--Has he made suitable proficiency in the preceding Degree?

S. D.--He has.

J. W.--And properly vouched for?

S. D.--He is.

J. W.--Who vouches for him?

S. D.--A brother.

J. W.--By what further right, or benefit does he expect to gain admission?

S. D.--By the benefit of the pass.

J. W.--Has he that pass?

S. D.--He has it not, but I have it for him.

J. W.--Advance and give me the pass.

Senior Deacon advances, and whispers in the Junior Warden's ear, "Shibboleth."

J. W.--The pass is right; I will suffer you to pass on to the Senior Warden's station in the west.

S. W.--Who comes here?

S. D.--Candidate, who has been regularly initiated Apprentice, and now wishes to receive more light in Masonry, by being passed to the Degree of Fellow Craft.

S. W. (turning to candidate.) --Candidate, is it of your own free-will and accord?

Candidate--It is, &c., &c.

Precisely the same questions and answers transpire as at the Junior Warden's station and at the door, and the candidate and Deacon are permitted by the Warden to pass to the Worshipful Master's station in the east.

W. M.--Who comes here?

S. D. (for candidate.) --Candidate, who has been regularly initiated Apprentice, and now wishes to receive more light in Masonry, by being passed to the Degree of Fellow Craft.

W. M.--(turning to candidate.) --Candidate, is it of your own free-will and accord?

Candidate. --It is.

W. M.--Brother Senior Deacon (the Master speaking in a very deep tone of voice), is he duly and truly prepared, worthy, and qualified?

S. D.--He is.

W. M.--Has he made suitable proficiency in the preceding Degree?

S. D--He has.

W. M.--And properly vouched for?

S. D.--He is.

W. M.--Who vouches for him?

S. D.--A brother.

W. M.--By what further right or benefit does he expect to gain admission?

S. D.--By the benefit of the pass.

W. M.--Has he that pass?

S. D.--He has it not. but I have it for him.

W. M.--Advance and give me the pass.

Senior Deacon advances, and whispers in the Master's ear, "Shibboleth."

W. M.--The pass is right; from whence came you, and whither are you travelling?

S. D.--From the west, travelling toward the east.

W. M.--Why leave you the west, and travel toward the east?

S. D.--In search of more light.

W. M.--Since that appears to be the object of the candidate's search, it is my orders that he be reconducted to the Senior Warden in the west, who will teach him how to approach the east, by two upright regular steps, his feet forming an angle of a square, his body erect at the altar before the Worshipful Master in the east.

Senior Deacon conducts the candidate back to the. Senior Warden in the west, and says:

S. D.--Brother Senior Warden, it is the orders of the Worshipful Master, that you teach this candidate to approach the east, by two upright regular steps, his feet forming an angle of a square, his body erect at the altar before the Worshipful Master in the east.

Senior Warden leaves his seat, and, approaching the candidate, he leads him toward the altar, and within two steps of it, and says:

Brother, you will first step off one full step with your left foot, bringing the heel of your right in the hollow of your left foot, now you will step off with your right foot, bringing the heel of your left in the hollow of your right. (Steps 1 and 2, Fig. 14, p. 93)

The candidate is now within kneeling distance of the altar, and the Senior Warden makes the following report to the Master: --

Worshipful Master, the candidate is now in order, and awaits your further will and pleasure.

W. M.--Brother Senior Warden, you will place him in due form for taking upon himself the solemn oath or obligation of a Fellow Craft.

The Senior Warden, with the assistance of the Senior Deacon, now causes the candidate to kneel on his naked right knee, before the altar, making his left knee form a square. His left arm, as far as the elbow, should be held in a horizontal position, and the rest of the arm in a vertical position, forming another square--his arm supported by the square, held under his elbow, and his right hand resting on the open Bible.

W. M.--Candidate, you are kneeling for the second time at the sacred altar of Masonry, to take upon yourself the solemn oath or obligation of a Fellow Craft; and I take pleasure, as Master of this Lodge, to say to you (as on a former occasion), there is nothing in this oath that will interfere with the duty that you owe to your God, your family, country, neighbor, or self. Are you willing to take it?

"Kneeling on my naked right knee, my left forming a square; my right hand on the Holy Bible, square, and compasses, my left arm forming an angle, supported by the square, and my hand in a vertical position."

Candidate--I am.

W. M.--Then, if you have no objections, you will say, I, and repeat your name after me (here the Master gives two raps with his gavel (• •), which is the signal for all the brethren to assemble around the altar).

OATH.

I, Candidate, of my own free-will and accord, in the presence of Almighty God, and this worshipful Lodge, erected to Him, and dedicated to the holy STS. JOHN, do hereby and hereon (Master presses candidate's hand with the gavel), most solemnly and sincerely promise and swear that I will always hail, and ever conceal, and never reveal any of the secret arts, parts, or points of the Fellow Craft Degree to any person whomsoever, except it be to a true and lawful brother of this degree, or in a regularly constituted Lodge of Fellow Crafts; nor unto him or them until, by strict trial, due examination, or lawful information, I shall find him, or them, as lawfully entitled to the same as I am myself.

I furthermore promise and swear that I will stand to, and abide by, all the laws, rules, and regulations of the Fellow Craft Degree, as far as the same shall come to my knowledge.

Further. I will acknowledge and obey all due signs and summons sent to me from a Lodge of Fellow Crafts, or given to me by a brother of that degree, if within the length of my cable-tow.

Further, that I will aid and assist all poor, distressed, worthy Fellow Crafts, knowing them to be such, as far as their necessities may require, and my ability permit, without any injury to myself.

Further, that I will not cheat, wrong, nor defraud a brother of this degree, knowingly, nor supplant him in any of his laudable undertakings.

All this I most solemnly promise and swear with a firm and steadfast resolution to perform the same, without any hesitation, mental reservation, or self-evasion of mind whatever, binding myself under no less penalty than of having my breast torn open my heart plucked out, and placed on the highest pinnacle of the temple (some say, My heart and vitals taken from thence, and thrown over my left shoulder, and carried into the valley of Jehoshaphat there to be devoured by the vultures of the air, should I ever knowingly violate the Fellow Craft obligation. So, help me God, and keep me steadfast in the due performance of the same.

W. M.--Candidate, you will detach your hand, and kiss the book on which your hand rests, which is the Holy Bible.

Candidate kisses the book.

W. M.--In your present condition, what do you most desire?

[60]*The candidate, prompted by his Deacon, answers--Lighter in Masonry.*

W. M.-Brethren, you will stretch forth your hands, and assist me in bringing our brother to light.

---

[60] The candidate is prompted here as in the E.A. He now better understands what he is in search for.

Here all the brethren place their hands in the form of the duegard of a Fellow Craft. (See Fig. 3, p. 17)

W. M.--Let the brother receive light.

At this point the Deacon unties the hoodwink, and lets it fall from the candidate's eyes. The Master then gives one rap on the altar with his gavel, when all the brethren but himself and the Deacon (S. D.) take their seats. The Master then says to the candidate:

W. M.--My brother, on being brought to light in this Degree, you behold one point of the compasses elevated above the square, which is to signify that you have received light in Masonry by points.

Then, stepping back a few feet from the altar, the Worshipful Master continues:

W. M.--Brother, you discover me approaching you from the east, under the duegard (here he makes the duegard) and sign (here he makes the sign of a Fellow Craft and In token of the continuance of brotherly love and favor, I present you with my right hand (takes candidate by the right hand), and with it the pass, token, token of the pass, grip, and word of a Fellow Craft. As you are yet uninformed, your Deacon will answer for you.

The Worshipful Master now takes the candidate by the Entered Apprentice's grip and says to his Deacon, the S.D., while holding the candidate by this grip:

W. M.--Here I left you. and here I find you. Will you be off or from?

S. D. (for candidate.) From.

W. M.--From what, and to what?

S. D.--From the real grip of an Entered Apprentice to the pass grip of a Fellow Craft.

W. M.--Pass.

Here the candidate is requested to pass his thumb from the first joint to the space between the first and second joints, which is the pass grip of a Fellow Craft.

W. M.--What is that?

Deacon--The pass grip of a Fellow Craft?

W. M.--Has it a name?

Deacon--It has.

W. M.--Will you give it to me?

Deacon--" Shibboleth." (Some letter it, Shib-bo-leth.)

W. M.--Will you be off or from?

Deacon-From.

W. M.--From what, and to what?

Deacon--From the pass grip of a Fellow Craft to the real grip of the same.

W. M. Pass.

W. M.--What is that?

Deacon--The real grip of a Fellow Craft.

W. M.--Has it a name?

Deacon--It has.

W. M.--Will you give it me?

Deacon--I did not so receive it, neither can I so impart it.

W. M.--How will you dispose of it?

Deacon--I will letter it or halve it.

W. M.--Halve it and begin.

Deacon. --No, you begin.

W. M.--Begin you.

Deacon. --Ja.

W. M.-Chin.

Deacon. --Jachin.

S. D.-Chin.

W. M.-Ja.

S. D.-Jachin.

W. M.--The pass is right. (At the words, "is right," lifting candidate from his knees at the altar.) You will rise and salute the Junior and Senior Wardens as Fellow Craft.

The Deacon having previously removed the cable-tow from the candidate's arm, he conducts him to the Junior Warden's station in the south, halts before that officer, and gives two raps on the floor with his rod, or stamps twice on the floor with his foot, which is responded to by the Junior Warden, in like manner, with his gavel.

J. W.--Who comes here?

Deacon--Candidate, an obligated Fellow Craft.

J. W.--How shall I know him to be such?

Deacon--By signs and tokens.

J. W.--Give me a sign.

Deacon gives the duegard of a Fellow Craft and makes the candidate or candidates--if there are more than one--do likewise.

J. W.--What is that?

Deacon--Duegard of a Fellow Craft Mason.

J. W.--Has it an allusion?

Deacon--It has; it alludes to the manner in which my hands were placed when I took upon myself the solemn oath of a Fellow Craft.

J. W.--Have you any other sign?

Deacon--I have. (At the same time, he makes the sign of a Fellow Craft, and the candidate does the same.)

J. W.--What is that?

Deacon--The sign of a Fellow Craft Mason.

J. W.--Has it an allusion?

Deacon--It has; it alludes to the penalty of my obligation.

J. W.--Have you any further signs?

Deacon--I have not; but I have a pass, token, token of the pass, grip, and word.

J. W.--Advance and give me the pass.

Warden takes hold of candidate by the right hand, and places his thumb on the first joint of candidate's hand and says to the Deacon:

J. W.--Will you be off or from?

Deacon--From.

J. W.--From what, and to what?

Deacon--From the real grip of an Entered Apprentice to the pass grip of a Fellow Craft.

J. W.--Pass.

J. W.--What is that?

Deacon--The pass grip of a Fellow Craft.

J. W.--Has it a name?

Deacon--It has

J. W.--Will you give it me?

Deacon--"Shibboleth."

J. W.--Will you be off or from?

Deacon-From.

J. W.--From what, and to what?

[61]Deacon--From the pass grip of a Fellow Craft to the real grip of the same.

J. W.--Pass.

J. W.--What is that?

Deacon--The real grip of a Fellow Craft.

J. W.--Has it a name?

Deacon--It has.

J. W.--Will you give it me?

Deacon--I did not so receive it, neither can I so impart it.

J. W.--How will you dispose of it?

Deacon--I will letter it or halve it.

J. W.--Halve it and begin.

Deacon--No, you begin.

J. W.--Begin you.

Deacon-Ja.

J. W.-Chin.

Deacon--Jachin.

---

[61] Note: A Pass grip and a real grip are not the same.

J. W.--The pass is right, and the word is right. I will suffer you to pass on to the Senior Warden's station in the west.

The Deacon and candidate now pass on to the Senior Warden in the west, where they pass precisely the same examination as that just described with the Junior Warden. The Senior Warden then permits them to pass on to the Worshipful Master in the east for his examination. As they (the candidate and Deacon) approach the master's station in the east, and when there, he (the Master) says:

W. M.--Brother Senior Deacon, you will reconduct the candidate to the Senior Warden in the west, with my orders that he teach him how to wear his apron as a Fellow Craft.

It should be here remarked, that when a candidate is prepared in the anteroom for the Fellow Craft's degree, he has an apron tied on him, with the flap up, as worn by an Entered Apprentice, which he wears until he arrives at this part of the ceremony.

The Deacon now conducts the candidate to the Senior Warden's station. This officer leaves his seat, and, approaching candidate, turns the flap of his apron down, at the same time saying--Brother, at the building of King Solomon's Temple, the Fellow

Crafts wore their aprons with the flap turned down and the corner turned up, and thus you will wear yours, until further advanced. (Tucks a corner under the string.)

FELLOW CRAFT'S APRON

The Deacon now reconducts the candidate to the Worshipful Master in the east.

W. M.--I now present you with the working tools of a Fellow Craft Mason, which are the plumb, square, and level.

The Master here shows the candidate these tools, which are generally made of rosewood .or ebony, and kept for these occasions on the Master's desk.

---

[62] One flap is up and tucked into top center. The significance of the F.C. apron is explained.

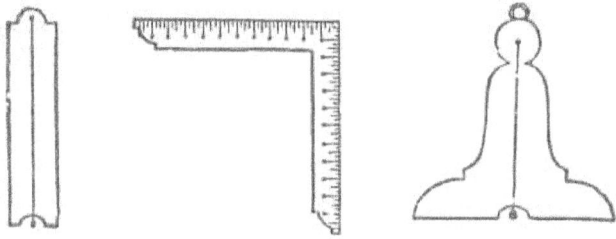

WORKING TOOLS OF A FELLOW CRAFT.

W. M.--The plumb is an instrument made use of by operative masons to raise perpendiculars.

W. M.--Brother Senior Deacon, it is my orders that you reconduct this candidate to the place from whence he came (ante-room), and invest him of what he has been divested of, preparatory to making an ascent through a porch, by a flight of winding stairs, consisting of three, five, and seven steps, to a place representing the Middle Chamber of King Solomon's Temple, there to receive instructions relative to the wages and jewels of a Fellow Craft.

The Deacon then leads the candidate to the center of the Lodge, before the altar, and makes the duegard and sign of a Fellow Craft, which is responded to by the Master. They then retire from the Lodge to the anteroom. After the candidate is out of the room, the Lodge is arranged for his second reception and the completion of the Degree. Two large pillars, each from six and a half to seven feet high, are

---

[63] The tools of a F.C.

placed near the door, about five feet apart, and fifteen pieces of painted board, of a rectangular

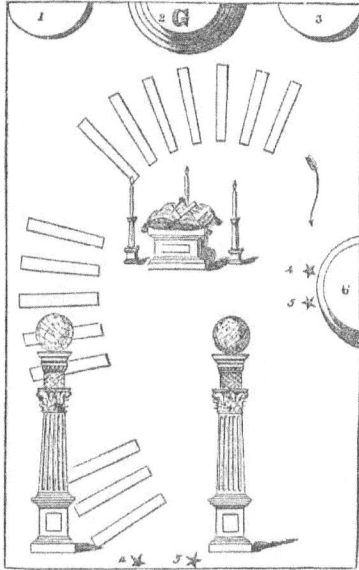

[65]REPRESENTATION OF THE CRAFTSMAN'S ROAD TO THE MIDDLE CHAMBER OF KING SOLOMON'S TEMPLE.

1. Treasurer 2. Worshipful Master. 3. Secretary. 4, 4. Deacon. 5, 5. Candidate. 6. Junior Warden.

form is arranged upon the carpet so as to represent three, five, and seven steps, or stairs. Some Lodges, especially those in the large cities, employ real steps, but in most

---

[64] The middle chamber is laid out here. Three, Five, and Seven step allude to different things.

[65] The middle chamber explained.

country Lodges the painted boards are used. For a more definite idea of this arrangement.

After the candidate is dressed, the Deacon ties upon him a white apron, with the flap turned down, as worn by Fellow Crafts. The Deacon then opens the Lodge-door, and, taking the candidate by the left arm, he leads him forward through the door in front of the pillars. For the first position of the parties see Fig. 13, the two stars representing the Deacon (i.e., S. D.) and the candidate.

Deacon--Candidate, we are now about to make an ascent through a porch, by a flight of winding stairs, consisting of three, five, and seven steps, to a place representing the Middle Chamber of King Solomon's Temple, there to receive instructions relative to the wages due, and jewels of a Fellow Craft.

[66]Masonry is considered under two denominations-- namely, Operative and Speculative. By Operative Masonry, we allude to the proper application of the useful rules of architecture, whence a structure will derive figure, strength, and beauty; and whence will result a due proportion and a just correspondence in all its parts. It furnishes us with dwellings, and convenient shelters from the vicissitudes and inclemencies of the seasons; and while it displays the effects of human wisdom, as well in the choice as in the arrangement of the sundry materials of which an edifice is composed, it demonstrates that a fund

---

[66] Modern Masonry practiced speculative masonry while our ancient brother practiced operative. We now use the tools for a more glorious purpose of developing the man into a better man.

of science and industry is implanted in man, for the best, most salutary, and beneficent purposes.

[67]By Speculative Masonry, we learn to subdue the passions, act upon the square, keep a tongue of good report, maintain secrecy, and practice charity. It is so far interwoven with religion as to lay us under obligations to pay that rational homage to the Deity, which at once constitutes our duty and our happiness. It leads the contemplative to view with reverence and admiration the glorious works of creation and inspires him with the most exalted ideas of the perfections of his Divine Creator.

[68]Our ancient brethren worked at both Operative and Speculative Masonry; they worked at the building of King Solomon's Temple, besides numerous other Masonic edifices. They wrought six days, but did not work on the seventh (7th), for in six days God created the heavens and the earth, and rested on the seventh day; therefore, our ancient brethren consecrated this day as a day of rest from their labors; thereby enjoying frequent opportunities to contemplate the glorious works of creation, and to adore their great Creator.

---

[67] We learn to improve ourselves in masonry by allegory and symbols.
[68] Our ancient brothers were Israelites. The Israelite rested on the seven days as commanded by God in the time of the Exodus. Shabbat was given as a gift to Israel. Though speculation about the identity of masons is debated it is clear based upon masonic teaching masons were the stone masons in ancient Israel. Solomon had Israelite masons who worked alongside Hiram of Tyre masons. Shabbat should be a part of a mason education as it was a part of our ancient institution.

[69]Brother, the first thing that particularly attracts our attention are (here the Deacon steps forward) two large brazen pillars (pointing at them with his rod), one on the right and one on the left hand. The name of the one on the left hand is Boaz and signifies strength; the name of the one on the right is Jachin, and denotes establishment; they, collectively, denote establishment and strength, and allude to a passage in Scripture: "In strength shall this house be established." These are representations of the two pillars erected at the outer porch of King Solomon's Temple. They are said to have been in height thirty-five (35) twelve in circumference, and four in diameter; they are said to have been adorned with two large chapiters of five cubits each, making their entire height forty (40) cubits. These chapiters were ornamented with a representation of net-work, lily-work, and pomegranates, and are said to denote Unity, Peace, and Plenty The network, from its connection, denotes unity; the lily-work, from its whiteness, and the retired place in which it grows, purity and peace; the pomegranates, from the exuberance of their seed, denote plenty. These chapiters have on the top of each a globe, or ball; these globes are two artificial spherical bodies; on the convex surfaces of which are represented the countries, seas, and various parts of the earth, the face of the heavens, the planetary revolutions; and are said to be thus extensive, to denote the universality of Masonry, and that a [70]Mason's charity ought to be equally extensive. The principal use of these globes, besides serving as maps, to distinguish the outward parts of the earth, and the situation of the fixed stars, is to illustrate and explain the

---

[69] Mason must understand the layout of the temple as explained here. The book of Kings describes this event.

[70] Tzedakah is the Hebrew word for charity which always represents justice. A mason charity should have no end as justice knows no end.

phenomena arising from the annual revolution and the diurnal rotation of the earth around its own axis. They are the noblest instruments for improving the mind and giving it the most distinct idea of any problem or proposition, as well as enabling it to solve the same.

[71]Contemplating these bodies, we are inspired with a due reverence for the Deity and his works and are induced to encourage the studies of astronomy, geography, navigation, and the arts dependent on them, by which society has been so much benefited.

The composition of these pillars is molten or cast brass; they were cast whole, on the banks of the river Jordan, in the clay grounds between SUCCOTH and ZAREDATHA, where King Solomon ordered these and all holy vessels to be cast.

They were cast hollow and were four inches or a hand's breadth thick. They were cast hollow the better to withstand inundation and conflagrations and are said to have contained the archives of Masonry.

Deacon-Brother, we will pursue our journey. (Stepping to the three steps on the floor or carpet.) The next thing that attracts our attention is the winding stairs which lead to the Middle Chamber of King Solomon's Temple, consisting of three, five, and seven steps.

---

[71] Contemplating the heavens will humble a human being as we realize how small we are compared to the endless heavens and their bodies. It incumbent upon the mason to study the sciences diligently so that he develops a well-founded foundation of knowledge.

[72]The first three allude to the three principal stages of human life, namely, youth, manhood, and old age. In youth, as Entered Apprentices, we ought industriously to occupy our minds in the attainment of useful knowledge; in manhood, as Fellow Crafts, we should apply our knowledge to the discharge of our respective duties to God, our neighbors, and ourselves; so that in old age, as Master Masons, we may enjoy the happy reflections consequent on a well-spent life, and die in the hope of a glorious immortality.

They also allude to the three principal supports in Masonry, namely, Wisdom, Strength. and Beauty; for it is necessary that there should be wisdom to contrive, strength to support, and beauty to adorn all great and important undertakings.

Stepping forward to the five steps, he continues:

The five steps allude to the five orders of architecture and the five human senses.

The five orders of architecture are Tuscan, Doric, Ionic, Corinthian, and Composite.

The five human senses are hearing, seeing, feeling, smelling, and tasting, the first three of which have ever been highly es-teemed among Masons: hearing, to hear the word; seeing, to see the sign; feeling, to feel the grip,

---

[72] Read and contemplate this section as it provides a blueprint of what to study.

whereby one Mason may know another in the dark as well as in the light.

The seven steps allude to the seven Sabbatical years, seven years of famine, seven years in building the Temple, seven golden candlesticks, seven wonders of the world, seven wise men of the east, seven planets; but, more especially, the seven liberal arts and sciences, which are grammar, rhetoric, logic, arithmetic, geometry, music, and astronomy. For this and many other reasons the number seven has been held in high estimation among Masons.

By this time, the Senior Deacon has passed the entire representation of the flight of stairs and is now at the Junior Warden's station in the south. Upon arriving here, he (the Senior Deacon) says to the candidate:

Brother, we are now approaching the outer door of King Solomon's Temple, which is tied or guarded by the Junior Warden. (Some say--our Junior Warden.)

As they approach the Junior Warden's desk, he (the Junior Warden) exclaims:

J. W.--Who comes here?

S. D.--A Craftsman, on his way to the Middle Chamber of King Solomon's Temple.

J. W.--How do you expect to gain admission?

S. D.--By the pass, and token of the pass of a Fellow Craft.

J. W.--Give me the pass.

S. D.--Shibboleth.

J. W.--What does that denote?

S. D.--Plenty.

T. W.--How is it represented?

S. D.--By ears of corn hanging near a water-ford.

J. W.--Why originated this word as a pass?

S. D.--In consequence of a quarrel which long existed between Jephthah, judge of Israel, and the Ephraimites: the latter had been a stubborn, rebellious people, whom Jephthah had endeavored to subdue by lenient measures, but to no effect. The Ephraimites, being highly incensed for not being called to fight, and share in the rich spoils of the Ammonitish war, assembled a mighty army, and passed over the river Jordan to give Jephthah battle; but he, being apprised of their approach, called together the men of Gilead, and gave them battle, and put them to flight; and, to make his victory more complete, he ordered guards to be placed on the different passes on the banks of the river Jordan, and commanded, if the Ephraimites passed that way, Say ye Shibboleth; but they, being of a different tribe, could not frame to pronounce it aright, and pronounced it Sibboleth; which trifling defect proved them to be spies, and cost them their lives; and there fell at that time, at the different passes on the banks of the river Jordan, forty and two thousand. This word was also used by our ancient brethren to distinguish a friend from a foe, and has since been adopted as a password, to be given before entering every regulated and well-governed Lodge of Fellow Crafts.

J. W.--Give me the token (here give the pass grip of a Fellow Craft).

J. W.--The pass is right, and the token is right; pass on.

They now pass around the Junior Warden's station, and go to the Senior Warden's Station in the west, and as they approach the Senior Warden's station the Senior Deacon remarks:

Brother, we are now coming to the inner door of the Middle Chamber of King Solomon's Temple, which is guarded by the Senior Warden in the west.

S. W.--Who comes here?

S. D.--A Craftsman, on his way to the Middle Chamber.

S. W.--How do you expect to gain admission?

S. D.--By the grip and word of a Fellow Craft.

S. W.--Give me the grip (here give the real grip of a Fellow Craft

S. W.--What is that?

S. D.--The real grip of a Fellow Craft.

S. W.--Has it a name?

S. D.--It has.

S. W.--Will you give it to me?

S. D.--I did not receive it, neither can I so impart it.

S. W.--How will you dispose of it?

S. D.--I will letter it or half it with you.

S. W.--Halve it and begin.

S. D.--No, you begin.

S. W.--Begin you

S. D.-Ja.

S. W.-Chin.

S. D.-Jachin.

S. W.--The word is right, and the grip is right; pass on, brother.

They pass on to the Worshipful Master in the east, and on their arrival at his desk, the Master rises from his seat, and says:

W. M.--Candidate, you have now arrived at the place representing the Middle Chamber of King Solomon's

Temple, where you will be received and recorded as a Fellow Craft. Turning to the Secretary's desk, he continues.

W. M.-Brother Secretary, you will make the record.

Sec--It is so recorded.

W. M.--The first thing that particularly attracted your attention on your passage here, was a representation of two brazen pillars, one on the left hand and the other on the right, which was explained to you by your Deacon; after passing the pillars you passed a flight of winding stairs, consisting of three, five, and seven steps, which was likewise explained to you; after passing the stairs, you arrived at the outer door of the Middle Chamber, which you found closely guarded by the Junior Warden, who demanded of you the pass and token of the pass of a Fellow Craft; you next arrived at the inner door of the Middle Chamber, which you found guarded by the Senior Warden, who demanded of you the grip and word of a Fellow Craft. You have now arrived at the Middle Chamber where you are received and recorded a Fellow Craft. You are now entitled to wages, as such, which are, the Corn of nourishment, the Wine of refreshment, and the Oil of joy, which denote peace, harmony, and strength. You are also entitled to the jewels of a Fellow Craft, which are an attentive ear, an instructive tongue, and faithful breast. The attentive ear receives the sound from the instructive tongue, and the mysteries of Masonry are safely lodged in the repository of faithful breasts.

[73]W. M.--I shall now direct your attention to the letter "G" which is generally placed on the wall back of the Master's seat and above his head; some Lodges suspend it in front of the Master, by a cord or wire), which is the initial of geometry, the fifth science, it being that on which this Degree was principally founded.

Geometry, the first and noblest of sciences, is the basis upon which the superstructure of Masonry is erected. By geometry, we may curiously trace nature through her various windings to her most concealed recesses. By it we discover the power, the wisdom, and the goodness of the Grand Artificer of the Universe, and view with delight the proportions which connect this vast machine. By it we discover how the planets move in their different orbits and demonstrate their various revolutions. By it we account for the return of the seasons, and the variety of scenes which each season displays to the discerning eye. Numerous worlds are around us, all formed by the same Divine Artist, and which roll through the vast expanse, and are all conducted by the same unerring law of nature. A survey of nature, and the observation of her beautiful proportions, first determined man to imitate the Divine plan, and study symmetry and order. This gave rise to societies, and birth to every useful art. The architect began to design, and the plans which he laid down, being improved by experience and time, have produced works which are the admiration of every age.

The lapse of time, the ruthless hand of ignorance, and the devastations of war have laid waste and destroyed many

---

[73] Here the F.C. learns the meaning of the "G" and how it is applied to the mason's life.

valuable monuments of antiquity on which the utmost exertions of human genius have been employed. Even the Temple of Solomon, so spacious and magnificent, and constructed by so many celebrated artists, escaped not the unsparing ravages of barbarous force. Freemasonry, notwithstanding, has still survived. The attentive ear receives the sound from the instructive tongue, and the mysteries of Masonry are safely lodged in the repository of faithful breasts. Tools and implements of architecture are selected by the fraternity, to imprint on the memory wise and serious truths; and thus, through a succession of ages, are transmitted unimpaired the excellent tenets of our institution.

W. M.--Candidate, this letter has a higher signification; it alludes to the sacred name of Deity (here he gives three raps with his gavel (• • •), when all in the Lodge rise to their feet), to whom we should all, from the youngest Entered Apprentice, who stands in the northeast corner, to the Worshipful Master, who presides in the east, with all sincerity humbly bow (here all bow their heads), with reverence most humbly bow. (Master gives one rap, when all the brethren take their seats again.)

W. M.-Candidate, this ends this degree, with the exception of a charge, which I will now give to you.

[74]CHARGE.

Brother: Being passed to the second degree of Masonry, we congratulate you on your preferment. The internal. and not the external qualifications of a man, are what Masonry regards.

As you increase in knowledge you will improve in social intercourse.

It is unnecessary to recapitulate the duties which, as a Mason, you are bound to discharge, or to enlarge on the necessity of a strict adherence to them, as your own experience must have established their value.

Our laws and regulations you are strenuously to support and be always ready to assist in seeing them duly executed. You are not to palliate, or aggravate, the offences of your

---

[74] The W.M. charges the F.C. as in the E.A.

Brethren: but, in the decision of every trespass against our rules, you are to judge with candor, admonish with friendship, and reprehend judge with justice.

The study of the liberal arts, that valuable branch of education, which tends so effectually to polish and adorn the mind, is earnestly recommended to your consideration--especially the science of geometry, which is established as the basis of our art. Geometry, or Masonry, originally synonymous terms, being of a divine and moral nature, is enriched with the most useful knowledge: while it proves the wonderful properties of nature, it demonstrates the more important truths of morality.

Your past behavior and regular deportment have merited the honor which we have now conferred; and in your new character it is expected that you will conform to the principles of the Order, by steadily persevering in the practice of every commendable virtue.

Such is the nature of your engagements as a Fellow Craft; and to these duties you are bound by the most sacred ties.

LECTURE ON THE FELLOW CRAFT DEGREE.

SECTION FIRST.

Q. Are you a Fellow Craft?

A. I am. Try me.

Q. How will you be tried?

A. By the square.

Q. Why by the square?

A. Because it is an emblem of morality, and one of the working-tools of my profession.

Q. What is a square?

A. An angle of ninety degrees, or a fourth part of a circle.

Q. Where did you make a Fellow Craft?

A. In a regularly constituted Lodge of Fellow Crafts.

Q. How were you prepared?

A. By being divested of all metals, neither naked nor clothed, barefoot nor shod, hoodwinked, with a cable-two twice about my right arm, in which condition I was conducted to the door of a Lodge by a brother.

Q. Why did you have a cable-two twice about your right arm?

A. To signify, as a Fellow Craft, that I was under a double tie to the fraternity.

Q. How did you get admission?

A. By three distinct knocks.

Q. To what do they allude?

A. To the three jewels of a Fellow Craft--an attentive ear an instructive tongue, and a faithful breast.

Q. What was said to you from within?

A. Who comes there.

Q. Your answer?

A. Brother A. B., who has been regularly initiated Entered Apprentice, and now wishes to receive more light in Masonry, by being passed to the degree of Fellow Craft.

Q. What were you then asked?

A. If it was of my own free-will and accord, if I was worthy and well qualified, duly and truly prepared, had made suitable proficiency in the preceding degree, and was properly vouched for; all of which being answered in the affirmative, I was asked by what further right or benefit I expected to gain admission.

Q. Your answer?

A. By the benefit of the pass.

Q. Did you give the pass?

A. I did not; but my Deacon gave it for me,

Q. What followed?

A. I was bid to wait with patience until the Worshipful Master should be informed of my request and his answer returned.

Q. What answer did he return?

A. Let him enter, in the name of the Lord, and be received in due form.

Q. How were you received?

A. On the angle of the square presented to my naked right breast, which was to teach me that the square of virtue should be the rule and guide of my conduct, in all my future transactions with mankind.

Q. How were you then disposed of?

A. I was conducted twice around the Lodge to the Junior Warden in the south, where the same questions were asked, and answers returned as at the door.

Q. How did the Junior Warden dispose of you?

A. He directed me to pass on to the Senior Warden in the west, and he to the Worshipful Master in the east, where the same questions were asked and like answers returned as before.

Q. How did the Worshipful Master dispose of you?

A. He ordered me to be returned to the Senior Warden in the west, who taught me to approach the east by two upright regular steps, my feet forming an angle of a square, my body erect at the altar before the Worshipful Master in the east.

Q. What did the Worshipful Master then do with you?

A. He made me a Fellow Craft in due form.

Q. What was that due form?

A. Kneeling on my naked right knee, my left forming a square, my right hand on the Holy Bible, square, and compasses, my left arm forming a right angle supported by the square in which due form I took the oath of a Fellow Craft. (Some repeat the oath.)

Q. After the obligation, what were you then asked?

A. What I most desired.

Q. Your answer?

A. Lighter in Masonry.

Q. Did you receive light?

A. I did, by the order of the Worshipful Master, and the assistance of the brethren.

Q. On being brought to light, what did you first discover, more than you had heretofore discovered?

A. One point of the compasses elevated above the square, which was to signify that I had received light in Masonry by points. Q. What did you then discover?

A. The Worshipful Master approaching me from the east, under the duegard and sign of a Fellow Craft; who, in token of the continuance of his brotherly love and favor, presented me with his right hand, and with it the pass, token, token of the pass, grip and word of a Fellow Craft, and ordered me to arise and salute the Junior and Senior Warden as such.

Q. After saluting the Wardens, what did you then discover?

A. The Worshipful Master ordered me to the Senior Warden in the west, who taught me to wear my apron as a Fellow Craft.

Q. How should a Fellow Craft wear his apron?

A. With the flap turned down, and the corner turned up.

Q. After being taught to wear your apron as a Fellow Craft, how were you then disposed of?

A. I was conducted to the Worshipful Master in the east, who presented me with the working-tools of a Fellow Craft (the plumb, square, and level), and taught me their use.

Q. What is their use?

A. The plumb is an instrument made use of, by operative masons, to raise perpendiculars; the square, to square their work; and the level, to lay horizontals. But we, as Free and Accepted Masons are taught to make use of them for more noble and glorious purposes: the plumb admonishes us to walk upright, in our several stations, before God and man; squaring our actions by the square of virtue; and remembering that we are travelling, upon the level of time, to "that undiscovered country from whose bourne no traveler returns."

Q. How were you then disposed of?

A. I was ordered to be returned to the place from whence I came, and invested of what I had been divested of, and was informed that, agreeably to an ancient custom in every well-governed Lodge, it therefore became necessary that I should make a regular ascent, by a flight of winding stairs, consisting of three, five, and seven steps, to a place representing the Middle Chamber of King Solomon's Temple, there to receive instructions relative to the wages and jewels of a Fellow Craft.

SECOND SECTION.

Q. Have you ever worked as a Fellow Craft?

A. I have, in speculative; but our forefathers wrought in both speculative and operative Masonry.

Q. Where did they work?

A. At the building of King Solomon's Temple, and of many other Masonic edifices.

Q. How long did they work?

A. Six days.

Q. Did they work on the seventh?

A. They did not.

Q. Why so?

[75]A. Because in six days God created the heavens and the earth and rested on the seventh day; the seventh day, therefore, our ancient brethren consecrated as a day of rest from their labors, thereby enjoying more frequent opportunities to contemplate the glorious works of creation and adore their great Creator.

Q. Did you ever return to the sanctum sanctorum, or holy of holies, or King Solomon's Temple?

A. I did.

Q. By what way?

A. Through a long porch or alley.

Q. Did anything in particular strike your attention to your return?

A. There did, viz.: two large columns, or pillars, one on the left hand, and the other on the right.

Q. What was the name of the one on the left hand?

A. Boaz, which denotes strength.

Q. What was the name of the one on the right hand?

A. Jachin, denoting establishment.

Q. What do they collectively allude to?

---

[75] The days of creation are described in Genesis.

A. A passage in Scripture, wherein God has declared in his word, "In strength shall this house be established."

Q. What were their dimensions?

A. Thirty-five cubits in height, twelve in circumference, and four in diameter.

Q. Where are they adorned with anything?

A. They were; with two large chapiters, one on each.

Q. What was the height of these chapiters?

A. Five cubits.

Q. Where are they adorned with anything?

A. They were; with wreaths of network, lily-work, and pomegranates.

Q. What do they denote?

A. Unity, Peace, and Plenty.

Q. Why so?

A. Network, from its connection, denotes union; lily-work, from its whiteness and purity, denotes peace; and pomegranates, from the exuberance of their seed, denote plenty.

Q. Were those columns adorned with anything further?

A. They were, viz.: with two large globes or balls, one on each.

Q. What was the entire height of these pillars?

A. Forty cubits.

Q. Did they contain anything?

A. They did, viz.: all the maps and charts of the celestial and terrestrial bodies.

Q. Why are they said to be so extensive?

A. To denote the universality of Masonry, and that a Mason's y ought to be equally extensive.

Q. What was their composition?

A. Molten or cast brass.

Q. Who cast them?

A. Our Grand Master, Hiram Abiff.

Q. Where were they cast?

A. On the banks of the river Jordan, in the clay ground between Succoth and Zaredatha, where King Solomon ordered these and all other holy vessels to be cast.

Q. Where do they cast solid or hollow?

A. Hollow.

Q. What was their thickness?

A. Four inches, or a hand's breadth.

Q. Why were they cast hollow?

A. The better to withstand inundations or conflagrations; they were said to contain all the archives of Masonry.

Q. What did you next come to?

A. A long, winding staircase, or flight of winding stairs, consisting of three, five, and seven steps.

Q. To what do the three steps allude?

A. The three principal supports in Masonry, namely: wisdom, strength, and beauty; they also allude to the three stages in human life: youth, manhood, and age; they further allude to the three degrees in Masonry: Entered Apprentice, Fellow Craft, and Master Mason.

Q. What do the five steps allude to?

A. The five orders in architecture, and the five-human sensed.

Q. What are the five orders in architecture?

A. The Tuscan, Doric, Ionic, Corinthian, and Composite.

Q. What are the five human senses?

A. Hearing, seeing, feeling, smelling, and tasting; the first three of which have ever been deemed highly essential among Masons: hearing, to hear the word; seeing, to see the sign; and feeling, to feel the grip, whereby one Mason may know another in the dark as well as in the light.

Q. What do the seven steps allude to?

A. The seven Sabbatical years, seven years of famine, seven years of war, seven years in building the Temple, seven golden candlesticks, seven wonders of the world, seven planets; but, more especially, the seven liberal arts and sciences, which are grammar, rhetoric, logic, arithmetic, geometry, music, and astronomy. For these and many other reasons the number seven has ever been held in high estimation among Masons.

Q. What did you next come to?

A. The outer door of the Middle Chamber of King Solomon's Temple, which I found partly open, but closely tyled by the Junior Warden in the south.

Q. How did you gain admission?

A. By the pass, and token of the pass of a Fellow Craft.

Q. What was the name of the pass?

A. SHIBBOLETH.

Q. What does it denote?

A. Plenty.

Q. How is it represented?

A. By ears of corn hanging near a water-ford.

Q. Why originated this word as a pass?

A. In consequence of a quarrel which had long existed between Jephthah, Judge of Israel, and the Ephraimites

Q. What did you next discover?

A. The inner door of the Middle Chamber of King Solomon's Temple.

Q. How did you gain admission?

A. By the grip and word of a Fellow Craft--Jachin.

Q. How did the Senior Warden dispose of you?

A. He ordered me to be conducted to the Worshipful Master in the east, who informed me that I had arrived at a place rep-resenting the Middle Chamber of King Solomon's Temple, where I would be received and recorded as such; which record was then made by the Secretary (by the orders of the Worshipful Master), and I was presented with the wages of a Fellow Craft, and also the jewels of a Fellow Craft.

Q. What are the wages of a Fellow Craft?

A. The corn of nourishment, the wine of refreshment, and the oil of joy.

Q. What do they denote?

A. Peace, harmony, and strength.

Q. What are the jewels of a Fellow Craft?

A. An attentive ear, an instructive tongue, and a faithful breast.

Q. How explained?

A. The attentive ear receives the sound from the instructive tongue, and the mysteries of Masonry are lodged in the repository of a faithful breast.

Q. What were you next shown?

A. The letter G.

Q. To what does it allude?

A. Geometry, the fifth science; but more particularly to the sacred name of the Deity, to whom we should all, from the Youngest Entered Apprentice who stands in the northeast corner, to the Worshipful Master who presides in the east, with reverence most devoutly and humbly bow.

This is the end of the Fellow Craft Degree, or Second Degree in Masonry.

MASTER MASON OR THIRD DEGREE.

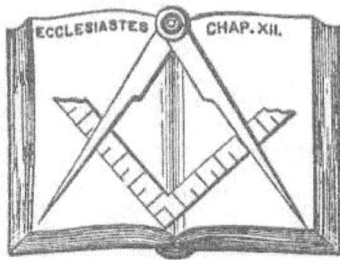

THE ceremony of opening and conducting the business of a Lodge of Master Masons is the same as in the Entered Apprentice and Fellow Crafts' Degrees, already explained. All the business of a "Blue Lodge" (a Lodge of three Degrees) is done in the Lodge while opened on this Degree, except that of entering an Apprentice or passing a

Fellow Craft, when the Lodge is lowered from the Masters'
Degree for that purpose.

The Third Degree is said to be the height of Ancient Free-
masonry, and the most sublime of all the Degrees in
Masonry (Royal Arch not even excepted); and when it is
conferred, the Lodge is well filled with the members of the
Lodge and visiting brethren.

The traditional account of the death, several burials, and
resurrections of one of the craft, Hiram Abiff, the widow's
son, as developed in conferring this Degree, is interesting.

We read in the Bible, that Hiram Abiff was one of the head
workmen employed at the building of King Solomon's
Temple, and other ancient writings inform us that he was
an arbiter between King Solomon and Hiram, king of Tyre;
but his tragical death is nowhere recorded, except in the
archives of Freemasonry. Not even the Bible, the writings of
Josephus, nor any other writings, however ancient, of which
we have any knowledge, furnish any information respecting
his death. It is very singular, that a man so celebrated as
Hiram Abiff was, universally acknowledged as the third
most distinguished man then living, and, in many respects,
the greatest man in the world, should pass from off the
stage of action, in the presence of King Solomon, three
thousand three hundred grand overseers, and one hundred
and fifty thousand workmen, with whom he had spent a
number of years, and with King Solomon, his bosom friend,
without any of his numerous confrères even recording his
death, or any thing

A Master Masons' Lodge is styled by the Craft the "Sanctum Sanctorum, or Holy of Holies, of King Solomon's Temple," and when the Lodge is opened on this Degree, both points of the compasses are elevated above the square. (See engraving.)

A candidate for the sublime Degree of a Master Mason is generally (as in the preceding Degrees) prepared by the Junior Deacon and the two Stewards, or some other brethren acting as such.

PREPARING THE CANDIDATE

The candidate is divested of all wearing apparel, except his shirt and drawers, and if he has not the latter, he is furnished with a pair by the brethren preparing him. The drawers are rolled up just above the candidate's knees, and both arms are taken out of his shirtsleeves, leaving his legs and breast bare. A rope, technically called, by Masons, a cable-tow, is wound around his body three times, and a bandage, or hoodwink, is tied very closely over his eyes. (See engraving.)

When the candidate is prepared, the Deacon takes him by the left arm, leads him up to the door of the Lodge, and gives three loud, distinct knocks.

The Senior Deacon, who has stationed himself at the inner door, at the right of the Senior Warden, on hearing these raps rises to his feet, makes the sign of a Master Mason to the Master, and says:

Worshipful Master, while engaged in the lawful pursuit of Masonry, there is an alarm at the inner door of our Lodge.

W. M.--You will address the alarm and ascertain the cause.

Senior Deacon gives three loud knocks (• • •), which are responded to by one (•) from the parties outside. The Senior Deacon then answers with one rap (•) and opens the door.

S. D.--Who comes here?

J. D.--Candidate, who has been regularly initiated Entered Apprentice, passed to the Degree of Fellow Craft, and now wishes to receive further light in Masonry, by being raised to the sublime Degree of a Master Mason.

S. D.-Candidate, is it of your own free-will and accord?

Candidate--It is.

S. D.--Brother Junior Deacon, is he worthy and qualified?

J. D.--He is.

S. D.--Duly and truly prepared?

J. D--He is.

S. D.--Has he made suitable proficiency in the preceding degrees?

J. D.--He has.

S. D.--And properly vouched for?

J. D.--He is.

S. D.--Who vouches for him?

J. D.--A brother.

S. D.--By what further right or benefit does he expect to gain admission?

J. D.--By the benefit of the password.

S. D.--Has he the password?

J. D.--He has it not, but I have it for him.

S. D.--Advance and give it me.

Junior Deacon here steps forward and whispers in the Senior Deacon's ear, "Tubal Cain."

S. D.--The pass is right; you will wait with patience until the Worshipful Master is informed of your request and his answer returned.

The Deacon then closes the door, repairs to the center of the Lodge-room before the altar, and sounds his rod on the floor three times (• • •), which is responded to by the Master with three raps of the gavel, when the Senior Deacon makes the sign of a Master Mason (see Fig. 6, p. 18.), and says:

S. D.--Candidate, who has been regularly initiated Entered Apprentice, passed to the Degree of Fellow Craft, and now wishes to receive further light in Masonry, by being raised to the sublime Degree of a Master Mason.

W. M.--Is it of his own free-will and accord?

S. D.--It is.

W, M.--Is he worthy and qualified, duly, and truly prepared?

S. D.--He is.

W. M.--Has he made suitable proficiency in the preceding degree?

S. D.--He has.

W. M.--And properly vouched for?

S. D.--He is.

W. M.--Who vouches for him?

S. D--A brother.

W. M.--By what further right or benefit does he expect to gain admission?

S. D.--By the benefit of the password.

W. M.--Has he that pass?

S. D.--He has it not, but I have it for him.

W. M.--Advance and give it me.

The Senior Deacon steps to the Master, and whispers in his ear, "Tubal Cain."

W. M.--The password is right. Let him enter and be received in due form.

The Senior Deacon steps to the altar, takes the compasses, repairs to the door, opens it, and says:

S. D.--Let him enter and be received in due form.

The Junior Deacon advances, followed by the Stewards, with rods, when the Senior Deacon stops them, by placing his hand against the candidate, at the same time saying:

S. D.--Candidate, on entering this Lodge the first time, you were received on the point of the compasses, pressing your naked left breast, the moral of which was explained to you. On entering the second time, you were received on the angle of the square, which was also explained to you. I now receive you on both points of the compasses, extending from your naked left to your naked right breast (he here places both points against candidate's breasts), which is to teach you, that as the vital parts of man are contained within the breasts, so the most excellent tenets of our institution are contained between the points of the compasses--which are Friendship, Morality, and Brotherly Love.

The Junior Deacon now passes the candidate over to the Senior

Deacon, and he (Junior Deacon) takes his seat near the door, at the right hand of the Senior Warden in the west, while the Senior Deacon proceeds to conduct the candidate, followed by the two Stewards, three times around the Lodge, during which time the Worshipful Master reads the following passage of Scripture:

"Remember now thy Creator in the days of thy youth, while the evil days come not, nor the years draw nigh when thou shalt say, I have no pleasure in them: while the sun, or the moon, or the stars be not darkened, nor the clouds return after the rain; in the day when the keepers of the house shall tremble, and the strong men shall bow themselves, and the grinders cease, because they are few; and those that look out of the windows be darkened, and the doors shall be shut in the streets, when the sound of the grinding is low, and he shall rise up at the voice of the bird, and all the daughters of music shall be brought low. Also when they shall be afraid of that which is high, and fears shall be in the way, and the almond-tree shall flourish, and the grasshopper shall be a burden, and desire shall fail; because man goeth to his long home, and the mourners go about the streets; or ever the silver cord be loosed, or the golden bowl be broken at the fountain, or the wheel at the cistern. Then shall the dust return to the earth as it was; and the spirit shall return unto God, who gave it."

As the Senior Deacon and candidate pass the different stations of the officers, they (the officers) sound their gavels as follows; when they pass the Junior Warden in the south the first time, he gives one rap (•), Senior Warden one rap, and Worshipful Master one rap; the second time,. Junior Warden two raps, Senior Warden two raps, and Worshipful Master two raps (• •); the third time round, Junior Warden three raps (• • •), Senior

Warden three raps, and the Worshipful Master three raps. The Master so times his reading of the passage of Scripture, as to finish just as the parties reach the Junior Warden's station in the south, on the third round, when they halt.

J. W.--Who comes here?

Deacon (S. D.) --Candidate, who has been regularly initiated Entered Apprentice, passed to the degree of Fellow Craft, and now wishes to receive further light in Masonry, by being raised to the sublime Degree of a Master Mason.

J. W.--Candidate, is it of your own free-will and accord?

Candidate--It is.

J. W.--Brother Senior Deacon, is he worthy and qualified, duly, and truly prepared?

S. D.--He is.

J. W.--Has he made suitable proficiency in the preceding Degrees?

S. D.--He has.

J. W.--And properly vouched for?

S. D.--He is.

J. W.--Who vouches for him?

S. D.--A brother.

J. W.--By what further right or benefit does he expect to gain admission?

S. D.--By the benefit of the password.

J. W.--Has he the password?

S. D.--He has it not, but I have it for him.

J. W.--Advance and give the password.

Senior Deacon steps forward, and whispers in the Warden's ear, "Tubal Cain."

J. W.--The password is right. I will suffer you to pass on to the Senior Warden's station in the west, for his examination.

Senior Deacon passes on to the west, where the same questions are asked and answered as before, and the Senior Warden suffers them to pass on to the Worshipful Master in the east, where the same questions and answers are repeated.

W. M.--From whence came you, and whither are you travelling?

S. D.--From the west, travelling toward the east.

W. M.--Why leave you the west, and travel toward the east!

S. D--In search of further light in Masonry.

W. M.--Since that is the object of your search, you will reconduct this candidate to the Senior Warden in the west, with my orders that he be taught to approach the east, the place of further light in Masonry, by three upright, regular steps, his body erect at the altar before the Worshipful Master in the east.

The Senior Deacon then conducts the candidate to the Senior Warden in the west, and reports:

S. D.--Brother Senior Warden, it is the orders of the Worshipful Master that you teach this candidate to approach the east, the place of further light in Masonry, by three upright, regular steps, his body erect at the altar before the Worshipful Master in the east.

The Senior Warden approaches the candidate, faces him toward the east (i.e. towards the Master), and says:

Brother, you will step off with your left foot one full step, and bring the heel of your right in the hollow of your left foot; now step off with your right foot, and bring the heel of your left in the hollow of your right foot; now step off with your left foot, and bring both heels together.

S. W.--The candidate is in order, Worshipful, and awaits your further will and pleasure.

W. M.--You will cause him to kneel on his naked knees, both hands resting on the Holy Bible, square, and compasses.

W. M.--Candidate, you are kneeling, for the third time, at the altar of Masonry, to take upon yourself the solemn oath of a Master Mason; and I, as Master of this Lodge, take pleasure, as on former occasions, in informing you that there is nothing in it which will interfere with the duty you owe to your God, your neighbor, your country, or self. Are you willing to take the oath?

"Kneeling on both my naked knees, both hands resting on the Holy Bible, square, and compasses."

Candidate--I am.

W. M.--You will repeat your name, and say after me:

"I, Candidate (Master gives three raps with his gavel, when all present assemble round the altar), of my own free-will and accord, in the presence of Almighty God, and this worshipful Lodge, erected to him and dedicated to the holy Sts. John, do hereby and hereon most solemnly and sincerely promise and swear, that I will always hail, ever conceal, and never reveal any of the secrets, arts, parts, point or points, of the Master Masons' Degree, to any person or persons whomsoever, except it be to a true and lawful brother of this Degree, or in a regularly constituted Lodge of Master Masons, nor unto him, or them, until by strict trial, due examination, or lawful information, I shall have found him, or them, as lawfully entitled to the same as I am myself.

"I furthermore promise and swear, that I will stand to and abide by all laws, rules, and regulations of the Master Masons' Degree, and of the Lodge of which I may hereafter become a member, as far as the same shall come to my knowledge; and that I will ever maintain and support the constitution, laws, and edicts of the Grand Lodge under which the same shall be holden.

"Further, that I will acknowledge and obey all due signs and summonses sent to me from a Master Masons' Lodge, or given me by a brother of that Degree, if within the length of my cable-tow.

"Further, that I will always aid and assist all poor, distressed, worthy Master Masons, their widows and orphans, knowing them to be such, as far as their necessities may require, and my ability permit, without material injury to myself and family.

"Further, that I will keep a worthy brother Master Mason's secrets inviolable, when communicated to and received by me as such, murder and treason excepted.

"Further, that I will not aid, nor be present at, the initiation, passing, or raising of a woman, an old man in his dotage, a young man in his nonage, an atheist, a madman, or fool, knowing them to be such.

"Further, that I will not sit in a Lodge of clandestine-made Masons, nor converse on the subject of Masonry with a clandestine-made Mason, nor one who has been expelled or suspended from a Lodge, while under that sentence, knowing him or them to be such.

"Further, I will not cheat, wrong, nor defraud a Master Mason's Lodge, nor a brother of this Degree, knowingly, nor supplant him in any of his laudable undertakings, but will give him due and timely notice, that he may ward off all danger.

"Further, that I will not knowingly strike a brother Master Mason, or otherwise do him personal violence in anger, except in the necessary defense of my family or property.

"Further, that I will not have illegal carnal intercourse with a Master Mason's wife, his mother, sister, or daughter, nor suffer the same to be done by others, if in my power to prevent.

"Further, that I will not give the Grand Masonic word, in any other manner or form than that in which I shall receive it, and then in a low breath.

"Further, that I will not give the Grand Hailing Sign of Distress, except in case of the most imminent danger, in a just and lawful Lodge, or for the benefit of instruction; and if ever I should see it given, or hear the words accompanying it, by a worthy brother in distress, I will fly to his relief, if there is a greater probability of saving his life than losing my own.

"All this I most solemnly, sincerely promise and swear, with a firm and steady resolution to perform the same, without any hesitation, mental reservation, or secret evasion of mind what-ever, binding myself, under no less penalty than that of having my body severed in two, my bowels taken from thence and burned to ashes, the ashes scattered before the four winds of heaven, that no more remembrance might be had of so vile and wicked a wretch as I would be, should I ever, knowingly, violate this my Master Mason's obligation. So, help me God, and keep me steadfast in the due performance of the same."

W. M.--You will detach your hands and kiss the book. In your present condition, what do you most desire?

Candidate (prompted by Deacon.)--Further light in Masonry.

W. M.--Let him receive further light.

Deacon here takes off the hoodwink and removes the cable-tow, and all around the altar place their hands in the position of the duegard of a Master Mason.

The Worshipful Master gives one rap with his gavel, when all the brethren retire to their seats, leaving at the altar the Master, Deacon, and candidate.

W. M.--Candidate, on receiving further light, you perceive more than you have heretofore. Both points of the compasses are elevated above the square, which is to teach you never to lose sight of those truly Masonic virtues, which are friendship, morality, and brotherly love.

The Master now steps back about three paces from the altar and says.

Candidate, you discover me approaching you from the east, under the duegard (some say--step, duegard, and sign) of a Master Mason; and, in token of the further continuance of my brotherly love and favor, I present. you with my right hand, and with it the pass and token of the pass of a Master Mason.

Takes the candidate by the "real grip" of a Fellow Craft and says.

Your Deacon will answer for you.

W. M.--Will you be off or from?

Deacon--From.

W. M.--From what and to what?

Deacon--From the "real grip" of a Fellow Craft to the pass grip of a Master Mason.

W. M.--Pass.

Deacon here instructs candidate to pass his thumb from the second joint to space beyond, which is the second space.

W. M. (looking Deacon in the eye.)--What is that?

Deacon--The pass grip of a Master Mason.

W. M.--Has it a name?

Deacon--It has.

W. M.--Will you give it me?

Deacon--I did not so receive it, neither can I so impart it.

W. M.--How will you dispose of it?

Deacon--I will letter it or halve it.

W. M.--Halve it and begin.

Deacon--No, you begin.

W. M.--Begin you.

Deacon--Tu.

W. M.--Bal.

Deacon--Cain. (Pronounced by the Deacon--Tubal Cain.)

W. M. (lifting the candidate up.)--You will arise and salute the Junior and Senior Wardens as an obligated Master Mason.

J. W.--Who comes here?

Deacon--Candidate, an obligated Master Mason.

J. W.--How shall I know him to be such?

Deacon--By the pass and token of the pass of a Master Mason.

J. W. (offering his hand to candidate.) --Advance the token. (They take hold of each other's hands by the real grip of a Fellow Craft. See the real grip of a Fellow Craft.

J. W.--Will you be off, or from?

Deacon (for candidate.) --From.

J. W.--From what, and to what?

Deacon--From the real grip of a Fellow Craft to the pass grip of a Master Mason.

J. W.--Pass. (They now pass to the pass grip of a Master Mason. (See Fig. 16, p. 97.)

J. W.--What is that?

Deacon--The pass grip of a Master Mason.

J. W.--Has it a name?

Deacon--It has.

J. W.--Will you give it me?

Deacon--I did not so receive it, neither can I so impart it.

J. W.--How will you dispose of it?

Deacon--I will letter or halve it.

J. W.--Halve it and begin.

Deacon--No, you begin.

J. W.--Begin you.

Deacon-Tu.

J. W.-Bal.

Deacon-Cain. (Pronounced by Deacon--Tubal Cain.)

J. W.--The token is right, and the pass is right. You will pass on to the Senior Warden's station in the west, for his examination.

They then pass on to this officer's station, where the same questions and answers are repeated as at the Junior Warden's station, and he (the Senior Warden) suffers them to pass on to the Worshipful Master's station in the east. As they approach the Worshipful Master's station, he says:

W. M.--Brother Senior Deacon, you will reconduct the candidate to the Senior Warden in the west, with my orders that he teach him how to wear his apron as a Master Mason.

The Deacon then turns about to the Senior Warden in the west, and says:

Brother Senior Warden, it is the orders of the Worshipful

Master that you teach this candidate how to wear his apron as a Master Mason.

The Senior Warden approaches the candidate and ties the apron upon him, with the flap and corners turned down, and says:

Master Masons wear their aprons

with the flap and corners
down, to designate them as
Master Masons, or as
overseers of the work, and
so you will wear yours.

76

A MASTER MASON'S APRON.

The Deacon now conducts
the candidate back to the
Worshipful Master in the east.

W. M.--Candidate, as you are clothed as a Master Mason, it
is necessary that you should have the working-tools or a
Master Mason. (Master has a small trowel, which he shows
the candidate as he commences to read concerning it.)

The working-tools of a Master Mason are all the
implements of Masonry appertaining to the first

three Degrees indiscriminately, but more especially the
trowel.

---

[76] M.M. apron – no flaps turned up.

[77]The trowel is an instrument made use of by operative masons to spread the cement which unites a building into one common mass; but we, as Free and Accepted Masons are taught to make use of it for the more noble and glorious purpose of spreading the cement of brotherly love and affection; that cement which unites us into one sacred band, or society of friends and brothers, among whom no contention should ever exist, but that noble contention, or rather emulation, of who best can work and best agree.

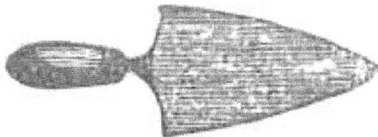

TROWEL.

W. M.--Brother Senior Deacon, you will now reconduct this candidate to the place from whence he came and reinvest him with what he has been divested of and await my further will and pleasure.

The Deacon then leads the candidate to the center of the Lodge, at the altar, and makes duegard and sign of a Master Mason which is responded to by the Master, after which the Deacon and candidate pass out of the Lodge. While they are going out, the Master gives three sounds with his gavel (• • •), and says, in a loud tone of voice:

---

[77] The trowel spreads brotherly love connecting multiple brothers into one unit.

W. M.-Brother Junior Warden, what is the hour? J. W.--High twelve, Worshipful.

W. M.--If you are satisfied it is high twelve, you will erect your column, and call the craft from labor to refreshment, for the space of thirty minutes (or fifteen minutes, as the case may be), calling them in at the sound of the gavel. On receiving this order, the Junior Warden takes from his desk a small wooden column, about eighteen inches in length, and sets it in an upright position at his right hand, and at the same time he gives three raps (• • •) with the gavel, and says:

J. W.-Brethren, you are accordingly at refreshment.

It should be remarked here that there is a similar column on the Senior Warden's desk, which is always placed in a horizontal position (i.e., turned down on its side) when the Junior Warden's column is up, and vice versâ. When the Lodge is opened, the Junior Warden's column is turned down, and the Senior Warden's turned up, at his right hand.

The brethren are now allowed a few minutes for recreation, styled by Masons refreshment; during which time, the candidate is being prepared in the anteroom, and the Lodge made ready for the remaining portion of the ceremony of initiation.

This latter is accomplished as follows: a canvas, seven feet long and about six feet wide, with five or six strong loops on each side, is produced from a closet or chest in the room; and a buckskin bag, stuffed with hair, about the size of two boxing-gloves, are taken from the same receptacle. These implements are both used as will be described hereafter.

The room is cleared by removing the altar and lights, and the two large pillars used in the Second Degree. By this time the candidate is dressed, his apron is tied on as a Master Mason, with the right-hand corner tucked up, and he wears a yoke with a Senior Warden's jewel attached to it. In some Lodges, the brethren on this occasion attire the candidate with a rich apron and yoke.

When the candidate is fully dressed, the door is unceremoniously thrown open, and he, in company with others, is permitted to enter the Lodge. His friends now approach him, and congratulate him upon his Masonic appearance, asking him how he likes the degree, and if he is not glad, he is through, &c., &c.

The object of this is to mislead the candidate, and to impress upon his mind the idea that there is no more of the ceremony, and that his initiation is completed.

Worshipful Master gives one rap with his gavel (•).

J. W.--Brethren, you are now called from refreshment to labor again. (Gives one rap (•), steps to his desk, and turns the small column down on its side, as already explained.)

At the same time, the Senior Warden steps to his stand and turns up the column on his desk to his right. The brethren then all take their seats, and the candidate with them.

W. M.--Brother Senior Warden, do you know any further business before this Lodge of Master Masons before we proceed to close?

S. W. (rising to his feet and making the sign of a Master Mason.) --Nothing, Worshipful.

W. M.--Have you anything to offer, Brother Junior Warden?

J. W. (making sign.) --Nothing, Worshipful.

W. M.--Have you anything on your desk, Brother Secretary?

Sec. (makes the sign, see Fig, 6, p. 18.) --Nothing, Worshipful.

W. M.--Has any brother present anything to offer for the benefit of Masonry? (Nothing being said, Worshipful Master continues): We will then proceed to close; but, before doing so, I would say to Candidate (the candidate) -- Is he present?

Some Brother--He is.

W. M.-Candidate, you will please approach the east.

Deacon (S. D.) leads the candidate up in front of the master's seat in the east.

After the candidate is conducted to the east, before the Master, the Deacon takes his position behind the candidate, with a hoodwink either in his hand or secreted in his pocket.

W. M. (looking candidate seriously in the face.) -- Candidate, I presume you now consider yourself a Master Mason, and, as such, entitled to all the privileges of a Master Mason, do you not?

Candidate--I do.

W. M.--I presumed that you did from the jewel that you wear, it being the Senior Warden's jewel.

W. M.--Candidate, you are not yet a Master Mason, neither do I know that you ever will be, until I know how well you will withstand the amazing trials and dangers that await you. The Wardens and brethren of this Lodge require a more satisfactory proof of your fidelity to your trust, before they are willing to entrust you with the more valuable secrets of this Degree. You have a rough and rugged road to travel, beset with thieves, robbers, and murderers; and should you lose your life in the attempt, it will not be the first instance of the kind, my brother. You will remember in whom you put your trust, with that divine assurance, that "he who endured unto the end, the same shall be saved." Heretofore you have had someone to pray for you, but now you have none. You must pray for yourself. You will therefore suffer yourself to be hoodwinked again, and kneel where you are, and pray orally or mentally, as you please. When through, signify by saying Amen, and arise and pursue your journey.

The candidate then kneels, and the Deacon ties a hoodwink very closely over both eyes, so that he cannot see.

After the candidate has said Amen, and the Lodge-room has been darkened by turning down the gaslights or lamps, the

The deacon takes the candidate by the right arm, assists him to arise, and they proceed to travel three times around the room, travelling with the sun. As they start, the Deacon commences to relate to the candidate the following:

Deacon--Brother, it was the usual custom of our Grand Master, Hiram Abiff (this is the first he hears about Hiram Abiff), to enter into the unfinished "Sanctum Sanctorum, or Holy of Holies," of King Solomon's Temple, each day at high twelve, while the craft were called from labor to refreshment, for the purpose of drawing out his designs upon the trestle-board, whereby the craft might pursue their labors; after which, it was further his custom to offer up his devotions to the Deity. Then he would retire at the south gate of the outer courts of the Temple; and, in conformity with the custom of our Grand Master, whose memory we all so reverently adore, we will now retire at the south gate of the Temple.

They have now passed around the Lodge three times, and as they approach the Junior Warden's station in the south, he steps silently out from his seat to the floor, and confronts the blind-folded candidate, clinching him by the collar in a very rough manner, and at the same time exclaiming:

left to right: S. D., or Deacon. Candidate. First Ruffian, Jubela, J. W. in the south.

J. W. (Jubela, First Ruffian.) --Grand Master Hiram, I am glad to meet you thus alone. I have long sought this opportunity. You will remember you promised us that when the Temple was completed, we should receive the secrets of a Master Mason, whereby we might travel in foreign countries, work, and receive master's wages. Behold! The Temple is now about to be completed, and we have not obtained what we have so long sought. At first, I did not doubt your veracity; but now I do! (Gives the candidate a sudden twitch by the collar.) I therefore now demand of you the secrets of a Master Mason!

Deacon (for candidate.) --Brother this is an unusual way of asking for them. It is neither a proper time nor place; but be true to your engagement, and I will be true to mine. Wait until the Temple is completed, and then, if you are found worthy and qualified, you will unquestionably receive the secrets of a Master Mason; but, until then, you cannot.

Ruffian--This (shaking candidate) does not satisfy me! Talk not to me of time or place, but give me the secrets of a Master Mason, or I will take your life!

Deacon--I cannot; nor can they be given, except in the presence of Solomon, king of Israel, Hiram, king of Tyre, and myself.

Ruffian--That does not satisfy me. I will hear no more of your caviling! (Clinches candidate more fiercely.) Give me the master's word, or I will take your life in a moment!

Deacon--I shall not!

The Ruffian gives the candidate a brush across the throat with his right hand, and at the same time relinquishes his hold with his left, steps quietly to one side, and permits the Deacon and candidate to pass on to the Senior Warden's station in the west, which is done by the Deacon advancing very rapidly, pulling the candidate along with him. As they approach the west, the Senior Warden steps out as did the Junior Warden, facing the candidate, and, clinching him by the collar more roughly than the Junior Warden, exclaiming as follows:

S. W. (Second Ruffian.) --Give me the secrets of a Master Mason!

Deacon (for candidate.) --I cannot.

Ruffian--Give me the secrets of a Master Mason! (Shakes candidate.)

Deacon--I shall not.

Ruffian--Give me the master's word, or I will take your life in a moment! (Gives candidate a sudden shake.)

Deacon--I will not!

Ruffian (i.e., S. W.) gives candidate a brush with his right hand across the left breast, and at the same time lets him pass, the Deacon hurrying him on toward the east end of the Lodge, where the Master is stationed to perform the part of the Third Ruffian, Jubelum, who is generally provided with a buckskin bag stuffed with hair, to represent a setting-maul.

As the candidate is hurried along toward Jubelum (Worshipful Master), the latter seizes him with both hands by the collar of his coat, and swings him round, so as to place his back toward the east, with his heels a few inches from the edge of the canvas before alluded to. This canvas is usually held behind the candidate, in an inclined position, by some of the brethren, and is for the purpose of catching him when he is tripped up by the assumed ruffian, Jubelum. The Master (Third Ruffian) then exclaims:

W. M. (as Third Ruffian.)--Give me the secrets of a Master Mason!

Deacon (for candidate.)--I cannot!

Ruffian--Give me the secrets of a Master Mason, or I will take your life!

Deacon--I shall not!

Ruffian--You have (here Master seizes the candidate more fiercely and affects a great earnestness of purpose) escaped "Jubela" and "Jubelo"; me you cannot escape; my name is "Jubelum!" What I purpose, that I perform. I hold in my hand an instrument of death; therefore, give me the Master's word, or I will take your life in a moment!

Deacon--I will not!

Ruffian--Then die!

Ruffian--Is he dead?

Answer--He is his skull is broken in.

Ruffian--What horrid deed is this we have done?

Answer--We have murdered our Grand Master, Hiram Abiff, and have not obtained that which we have sought: this is no time for vain reflection--the question is, what shall we do with the body?

Answer--We will bury it in the rubbish of the Temple until low twelve, and then we will meet and give it a decent burial.

Answer--Agreed!

First Ruffian--Is that you, Jubela?

Answer--Yes.

Second Ruffian--Is that you, Jubelum?

Answer--Yes.

Third Ruffian--Is that you, Jubelo?

Answer--Yes.

First Ruffian--Well, we have all met as agreed upon: the question is, what shall we do with the body? It is now past midnight, and if we do not decide, daylight will be upon us, and we will be discovered and taken. We will carry the body a westerly course from the Temple to the brow of the hill west of Mount Moriah, where I have dug a grave due east and west, six feet perpendicular.

Answer--Agreed!

A sufficient number of the brethren now accept the body (yet rolled up in the canvas), and, raising it on their shoulders, proceed to carry it around the Lodge, head foremost, three times, in representation of ascending a hill, the last time halting in the west end of the Lodge, nearly in front of the Senior Warden's station, and a little to the right. Upon arriving there they commence to lower it into the grave, as they style it, but in reality, only from their shoulders to the floor. After the candidate is lowered, one of the ruffians says:

Let us plant an acacia at the head of the grave, in order to conceal it so that the place may be known should occasion hereafter require.

Some Lodges have a small box with a houseplant or dry twig in it, which is set down on the floor near the candidate's head. One of the ruffians exclaims:

Now let us make our escape out of the country.

First Ruffian--Hallo, friend! Are you a sea-captain?

Captain--I am.

Second Ruffian--Are you going to put to sea soon?

Captain--Immediately.

Third Ruffian--Whither are you bound?

Captain--To Ethiopia.

Ruffian--The very port to which we wish to go. We three should like to take a passage with you.

Captain--Very well, you can have a passage. I suppose you are brothers, workmen from the Temple, and journeying, are you not?

Ruffians--We are.

Captain--I should be glad of your company. Do you have a pass from King Solomon, I presume?

Ruffians (affecting surprise.) --No, we have no pass; we did not know it was necessary. We were sent in haste and on urgent business; there was nothing said about giving us a pass, and we presume it was forgotten, or not deemed necessary.

Captain--What! no pass. What! no pass. If this is the case, you cannot get a passage with me, I assure you. That is forbidden; so, you may set your minds at rest.

Ruffians--We will go back and get a pass if that is the case.

Captain--The sooner the better! Suspicious characters!

The Ruffians now return near to the body when the following conversation takes place:

First Ruffian--What shall we do in this case?

Second Ruffian--We will go to some other port.

Third Ruffian--But the rules are as strict in other ports as in this.

First Ruffian--If such are the regulations, we shall not get a pass at any port, and what will become of us?

Second Ruffian--We shall be taken and put to death.

Third Ruffian--Let us secrete ourselves until night and steal a small boat and put it to sea.

First Ruffian--We cannot make our escape in that way. It is a dangerous coast, and we shall be taken; for before this time our escape is discovered, and the seacoast will be lined with our pursuers.

Second Ruffian--Then let us flee into the interior parts of the country and avoid being taken as long as possible.

Third Ruffian--Agreed!

No work today. Craftsmen, we are having good times; I wonder if it will last.

W. M. (now styled King Solomon.) --Brother Junior Grand Warden, what means all this confusion among the workmen? Why are they not at work as usual?

S. W. (now styled J. G. W.) --Most Worshipful King Solomon, there is no work laid out for us, and it is said we can have none. No designs are drawn on the trestle-board, and for this reason many of us are idle.

K. S.--No work laid out--no designs drawn on the trestle-board? What is the meaning of this? Where is our Grand Master, Hiram Abiff?

J. G. W.--We do not know, Most Worshipful King Solomon. He has not been seen since high twelve yesterday.

K. S.--Not been seen since high twelve yesterday! I fear he is indisposed. It is my orders that strict search be made for him through the apartments of the Temple, and due inquiry made. Let him be found, if possible.

The brethren commence, in loud voices to inquire of one another:

Have you seen anything of our Grand Master Hiram Abiff? Not since high twelve yesterday, &c., &c.

J. G. W.--Most Worshipful King Solomon, diligent search has been made. He cannot be found. He has not been seen in or about the Temple.

K. S.--I fear that some accident has befallen him. Brother Grand Secretary (turning to the Secretary of the Lodge), you will go out and see to calling the several rolls of the craft, and report to me as soon as possible.

G. Sec.--Assemble, Craftsmen! It is King Solomon's orders that the several rolls be called, and report made as soon as possible.

G. Sec.--Most Worshipful King Solomon, the several rolls have been called, and reports made, by which it appears that three Fellow Crafts are missing, namely, Jubela, . Jubelo, and Jubelum, who, from the similarity of their names, I presume are brothers, and men from Tyre.

J. G. W.--Most Worshipful King Solomon, there are at the gate twelve Fellow Crafts, who wish to be admitted: they say they come with important tidings.

K. S.--Let them be admitted.

Here the Warden opens the ante-room door, and says: "Come in, you twelve Fellow Crafts;" when all those that were left out by the Secretary come into the Lodge, stamping and scuffling along, especially if only a few of them, to impress upon the candidate's mind the idea that there are more. They advance before the Master in the east, and form across the Lodge, when all make the duegard and sign of a Fellow Craft (Figs. 3 and p. 17) which is responded to by the Master. Then one of the best posted relates the responded following, in a clear and distinct voice:

"Most Worshipful King Solomon, we come to inform you that fifteen of us Fellow Crafts, seeing the Temple about to be completed, and being desirous of obtaining the secrets of a Master Mason, by which we might travel in foreign countries, and receive Master's wages, entered into a horrid conspiracy to extort them from our Grand Master,

Hiram Abiff, or take his life; but, reflecting with horror on the atrocity of the crime, twelve of us recanted; but the other three persisted in their murderous design, and we fear that they have taken the Grand Master's life. We therefore now appear before your Majesty, clothed with white gloves and aprons, in token of our innocence, and, acknowledging our premeditated guilt, we humbly implore your pardon." (They all kneel.)

K. S.--Arise, you twelve Fellow Crafts, divide yourselves into parties and travel--three east, three north, three souths, and three west--with others whom I shall appoint, in search of the ruffians.

The brother who has acted the part of sea-captain now takes his station at the door again, when these Fellow Crafts approach him in the west.

First Craftsman--Hallo, friend! have you seen any strangers pass this way?

Capt.--I have three.

Craftsman--Describe them if you please.

Capt.--They were three brothers, workmen from the Temple, seeking a passage to Ethiopia, but not having King Solomon's pass, were not able to obtain one, and returned back into the country.

Second Craftsman--The very fellows of whom we are in pursuit. Did you say they turned back into the country?

Capt.--Yes.

Craftsman--We will go in pursuit of them; they are the fellows we want. (Moving off, one says:)

Let us report.

And at the same time, he steps to the Master's desk, and re-ports as follows:

"Most Worshipful King Solomon, I, being one of those who pursued a westerly course, coming down near the port of Joppa, met a seafaring man, of whom I inquired if he had seen any strangers pass that way; he informed me that he had--three--who from their appearance were workmen from the Temple, seeking a passage to Ethiopia, but not having King Solomon's pass, were not able to obtain one, and returned back into the country.

K. S.--Divide yourselves and travel, as before, with positive instructions to find the ruffians, and with as positive assurance that, if you do not, the twelve shall be deemed the murderers, and suffer severally, for the crime committed.

They now separate about the Lodge, saying to each other:

"This is very unjust of the King. We are told if we do not find the ruffians we must be punished--put to death. What have we done? It is true, we have been associated with these three ruffians, but we have not committed any actual crime"

By this time, they have near the candidate (who is still lying on the floor, rolled up in the canvas), when one of the parties sits down near his head, and at the same time says:

"Well, brothers, I am very weary; I must sit down and rest before I can go any farther."

One of his companions exclaims: "I am tired, too!" and sits down near the candidate.

Another says: "What course shall we pursue? we must not go and report ourselves; if we do, the twelve will be put to death. Here are three of the poor fellows with us; we must not go and give them up, to be put to death; let us take a northwesterly or a southwesterly course. Which way shall we go?"

One of the brethren then replies: "We will go a southwesterly course and will come up with our brothers." Attempting to get up, he exclaims, "Hallo! what's this?" at the same time pulling up the evergreen--or acacia, as it is styled--at the head of the grave. "What makes this acacia coming up so easily? The ground has been newly broken; this has the appearance of a grave," pointing to the candidate on the floor.

One of the brothers, representing one of the three ruffians, in a corner nearby, is now heard to exclaim, in a loud, but deep tone of voice:

"Oh! that my throat had been cut across, my tongue torn out by its roots, and buried in the rough sands of the sea, at low-water mark, where the tide ebbs and flows twice in twenty-four hours, ere I had been accessory to the death of so good a man as our Grand Master, Hiram Abiff."

"Hark! that is the voice of Jubela."

"Oh! that my breast had been torn open, my heart plucked out, and placed upon the highest pinnacle of the Temple, there to be devoured by the vultures of the air, ere I had consented to the death of so good a man as our Grand Master, Hiram Abiff."

"Hark! that is the voice of Jubelo."

"Oh! that my body had been severed in two, my bowels taken from thence and burned to ashes, the ashes scattered to the four winds of heaven, that no more remembrance could be had of so vile and wicked a wretch as I. Ah! Jubela, Jubelo, it was I that struck him harder than you both: it was I that gave him the fatal blow; it was I that killed him."

"That is the voice of Jubelum."

The three craftsmen, having stood by the candidate all this time, listening to the ruffians, whose voices they recognize, say one to another:

"What shall we do? There are three of them, and only three of us."

One says:

Our cause is just; let us rush in and seize them."

Upon which the three Fellow Crafts rush forward over benches and chairs, and secure the ruffians in no very gentle manner, and lead them to the Worshipful Master's seat in the east, when one of them reports to the Master:

"Most Worshipful King Solomon, I, being one who pursued a westerly course, and, on my return, after several days of fruit-less search, being more weary than my companions, sat down on the brow of a hill to rest and refresh myself; and, on rising, accidentally caught hold of a sprig of acacia, which, easily giving way, excited my suspicions. Having my curiosity aroused, I examined it, and found it to be a grave."

As soon as the craftsman has finished this report, another party arrives with the ruffians, and reports as follows:

"Most Worshipful King Solomon, while sitting down to rest and refresh ourselves, we heard the following horrid exclamations from the clefts of the adjacent rocks. The first was the voice of Jubela exclaiming: 'Oh! that my throat had been cut across, my tongue torn out by its roots, and buried in the rough sands of the sea, at low-water mark, where the tide ebbs and flows twice in twenty-four hours, ere I had been accessory to the death of so good a man as our Grand Master, Hiram Abiff.' The second was that of Jubelo, exclaiming: 'Oh! that my breast had been torn open, my heart plucked out and placed upon the highest pinnacle of the Temple, there to be devoured by the vultures of the air, ere I had consented to the death of so good a man as our Grand Master, Hiram Abiff.' The third was the voice of Jubelum, exclaiming, louder than the rest: 'It was I that gave the fatal blow, it was I that killed him. Oh! that my body had been severed in two, my bowels taken from thence, and burned to ashes, the ashes scattered to the four winds of heaven, that no more remembrance might be had of so vile and wicked a wretch as I. Ah! Jubela! Jubelo! it was I that struck him harder than you both; it was I that gave him the fatal blow; it was I that killed him.' Upon which we rushed in, seized and bound the ruffians, and now have them before your majesty."

K. S.--Jubela, you stand charged as accessory to the death of our Grand Master, Hiram Abiff. What say you, guilty or not guilty?

One answers, in a very penitent manner:

Guilty, my lord.

K. S.--Jubelo, you also stand accessory to the death of our Grand Master, Hiram Abiff. What say you, sir, guilty or not guilty?

Answer--Guilty, my lord.

K. S.--Jubelum, you stand charged as the willful murderer of our Grand Master, Hiram Abiff. What say you, sir, guilty or not guilty?

Answer--Guilty, my lord.

K. S.--Vile, impious wretches! despicable villains! Reflect with horror on the atrocity of your crime, and on the amiable character of your Worshipful Grand Master, whom you have so basely assassinated. Hold up your head and hear your sentence. It is my orders that you be taken without the gates of the court, and be executed, according to your several imprecations, in the clefts of the rocks. Brother Junior Grand Warden, you will see my orders duly executed. Begone!

They all pass out of the Lodge with a rush, into the anteroom, where they form into a circle. One, acting as the principal mover, raises his right foot from the floor, at the same time his hands, in the manner of slapping them together, makes two false motions, but at the third all bring down their right feet and hands together, producing a very sharp noise. A momentary silence then ensues, during which one of the party groans, as if nearly dying. This is all intended to produce its effect upon the ears of the candidate. It also represents the execution and dying groans of Jubela, the first ruffian, and is repeated twice more to represent the death of the other two ruffians. Some Lodges use a large drum, others roll a large cannonball across the ante-room floor, letting it strike on a cushion placed against the wall. This is not, however, practiced in city Lodges.

The ruffians being executed, the brethren all return quietly to the Lodge, when one of them reports, in a loud tone of voice:

"Most Worshipful King Solomon, your orders have been duly executed upon the three murderers of Grand Master, Hiram Abiff."

K. S.--You twelve Fellow Crafts will go in search of the body, and, if found, observe whether the master's word, or a key to it, or anything that appertains to the Master's Degree, is on or about it.

The brethren representing the twelve repentant conspirators now walk out near the spot where the candidate is lying, and, when close to him, one of the parties says:

"Well, brothers, can we find where the acacia was pulled up?"

Approaching the candidate, another replies:

"Yes, this is the place; let us remove the rubbish and dig down here."

A third, lifting up the canvas, says:

"Yes, here is the body of our Grand Master, Hiram Abiff, in a mangled and putrid state. Let us go and report. But what were our orders? We were ordered to observe whether the Master's word, or a key to it, or anything appertaining to the Master's Degree, was on or about the body; but, brothers, we are only Fellow Crafts, and know nothing about the Master's word, or a key to it, or anything appertaining to the Master's

Degree; we must, however, make an examination, or we will be put to death."

They then commence to search about the candidate, lifting off the canvas, feeling about his neck, &c., &c.: finally, one of the brethren, taking hold of the jewel which is attached to the yoke about the candidate's neck, exclaims:

"This is the jewel of his office."

Another says:

"Let us go and report that we find nothing on or about the body excepting the jewel of his office."

One of the brothers now takes off the jewel from the candidate's neck, and all repair to the master's seat in the east, and report:

"Tidings of the body."

K. S.--Where was it found?

Answer--A westerly course, where our weary brother sat down to rest and refresh himself.

K. S.--Was the master's word, or a key to it, or anything appertaining to the Master's Degree, on or about it?

Answer--Most Worshipful King Solomon, we are but Fellow Crafts; we therefore know nothing about the master's word or the Master's Degree. There was nothing found on or about the body excepting the jewel of his office, by which his body was discovered.

They present the jewel to the Master, who, on examination of it, says:

"This is the jewel of our Grand Master, Hiram Abiff; there can be no longer any doubt as to the identity of the body."

K. S.--You twelve Fellow Crafts will now go and assist in raising the body.

Turning in his seat toward the Treasurer's desk, he says to the Treasurer:

"My worthy brother of Tyre, as the master's word is now lost, the first sign given at the grave, and the first word spoken, after the body is raised, shall be adopted for the regulation of all Masters' Lodges, until future generations shall find out the right."

Treasurer--Agreed.

All now form in a circle around the body, the Master, and Wardens at the head, when the Master makes the sign of "distress" of a Master Mason, which is done by raising both hands and arms above the head. (See grand hailing sign of distress, Fig. 7, p. 18.) As the Master makes this sign, he says:

"O Lord my God, I fear the Master's word is forever lost!"

Sol - emn strikes the fu - neral chime, Notes of

our de - part - ing time; As we jour - ney here be -

low, Through a pil - grim - age of woe!

"Solemn strikes the funeral chime,
Notes of our departing time;
As we journey here below,
Through a pilgrimage of woe!"

"Mortals, now indulge a tear,
For Mortality is here:

See how wide her trophies wave
O'er the slumbers of the grave!

III.

"Here is another guest we bring.
Seraphs of celestial wing,
To our funeral altar come:
Waft this friend and brother home.

IV.

"Lord of all! below--above--
Fill our hearts with truth and love;
When dissolves our earthly tie,
take us to thy Lodge on High."

*Master (as K. S.) makes the "grand hailing sign of distress"
some master's make this sign twice), accompanied by the
following exclamation, viz.: "O Lord my God, I fear the
Master's word is forever lost!" He then turns to the Junior
Warden and says: "You will take the body by the Entered
Apprentice grip and see if it can be raised."*

*The Junior Warden then takes hold of the candidate's right
hand, giving him the Entered Apprentice's grip and then lets
his hand slip off in a careless manner, and reports:*

"Most Worshipful King Solomon, owing to the high state of putrefaction, it is, having been dead already fifteen days, the skin slips, and the body cannot be raised."

K. S. (making grand hailing sign of distress.) --O Lord my God, I fear the Master's word is forever lost!

K. S.--My worthy brother of Tyre, I will thank you for endeavoring to raise the body by the Fellow Craft's grip.

The Senior Warden then takes the candidate's right hand, giving the real grip of a Fellow Craft (see Fig. 12, p. 67), and letting his hand slip off quickly, he reports as follows:

"Owing to the reason before given, the flesh cleaves from the bone, and the body cannot be so raised."

K. S.--O Lord my God! O Lord my God!! O Lord my God!!!!! Is there no hope for the widow's son?

At each exclamation he gives the grand hailing sign of distress, which would be three times, then, turning to the Senior Warden, says:

"My worthy brother of Tyre, what shall we do?"

S. W.--Let us pray.

The brethren now all kneel around the body on one knee. The Master kneels at the head of the candidate, and, taking off his hat, repeats the following prayer, which may be found in all the Masonic Monitors:

PRAYER.

Thou, O God! knows our down sitting and our uprising and understands our thoughts from afar off. Shield and defend us from the evil intentions of our enemies and support us under the trials and afflictions we are destined to endure, while travelling through this vale of tears. Man, that is born of a woman is of few days and full of trouble. He cometh forth as a flower and is cut down: he flees also as a shadow and continued not. Seeing his days are determined, the number of his months are with thee; thou hast appointed his bounds that he cannot pass; turn from him that he may rest, till he shall accomplish his day. For there is hope of a tree, if it is cut down, that it will sprout again, and that the tender branch thereof will not cease. But man, dies and waste away; yes, man giveth up the ghost, and where is he? As the waters fail from the sea, and the flood decayed and dried up, so man lieth down, and rises not up till the heavens shall be no more. Yet, O Lord! have compassion for the children of their creation, administer them comfort in time of trouble, and save them with everlasting salvation. Amen.

Response--So mote it be.

All the brethren now rise to their feet.

K. S. (to the S. W.) --My worthy brother of Tyre, I shall endeavor (with your assistance) to raise the body by the strong grip, or lion's paw, of the tribe of Judah. (See Fig. 17.)

The Master steps to the feet of the candidate, bending over, takes him by the real grip of a Master Mason, places his right foot against the candidate's right foot, and his hand to his back, and, with the assistance of the brethren, raises him up perpendicularly in a standing position, and, when fairly on his feet, gives him the grand Masonic word on the five points of fellowship. (See Fig. 18.) In the meantime, the canvas is slipped out of the Lodge, and as the Master commences to give or whisper the word in the candidate's ear, one of the brethren slips off the hoodwink, and this is the first time he has seen light in an hour. The following is the representation of the Master giving candidate the grand Masonic word, or at least this is a substitute, for, according to Masonic tradition, the right one was lost at the death of Hiram Abiff. This word cannot be given in any other way, and by Masons is considered a test of all book Masons.

The Master having given the word, which is MAH-HAH-BONE, in low breath, requests the candidate to repeat it with him, which is in this wise:

Master whispers in candidate's ear--Mah.

Candidate--Hah.

Master-Bone.

Master telling candidate never to give it in any other way than that in which he has received it. The Master, stepping back one pace, now says:

"Candidate, you have now received that grand Masonic word, which you have solemnly sworn never to give in any other way or form than that in which you have received it, which is on the five points of fellowship, and then in low breath. (See page 247.)

'The five points of fellowship are--foot to foot, knee to knee, breast to breast, hand to back, and cheek to cheek, or mouth to ear.

It is done by putting the inside of your right foot to the inside of the right foot of the one to whom you are going to give the word, the inside of your own knee to his, laying your breast close against his, your left hands on each other's back, and each one putting his mouth to the other's right ear.

Five Point of Fellowship

"1st. Foot to foot--that you will never hesitate to go on foot, and out of your way, to assist and serve a worthy brother.

"2nd. Knee to knee--that you will ever remember a brother's welfare, as well as your own, in all your adorations to Deity.

"3d. Breast to breast--that you will ever keep in your breast a brother's secrets, when communicated to and received by you as such, murder and treason excepted.

"4th. Hand to back--that you will ever be ready to stretch forth your hand to assist and save a fallen brother; and that you will vindicate his character behind his back, as well as before his face.

"5th. Cheek to cheek, or mouth to ear--that you will ever caution and whisper good counsel in the ear of an erring brother, and, in the friendliest manner, remind him of his errors, and aid his reformation, giving him due and timely notice, that he may ward off approaching danger."

All the brethren take their seats but the Master and candidate when the Master continues:

"Candidate, you will now repair to the east, and receive an historical account of this degree."

Master now takes his seat in the east, and requests candidate to stand before him.

[78]HISTORICAL ACCOUNT.

W. M.--Candidate, the second section of this degree exemplifies an instance of virtue, fortitude, and integrity seldom equaled, if ever excelled, in the history of man.

You have this evening represented one of the greatest men, and the greatest Mason, the world ever knew, viz., our Grand Master, Hiram Abiff, who was slain just before the completion of King Solomon's Temple. His death was premeditated by fifteen Fellow Crafts, who, seeing the Temple about to be completed, and being desirous of obtaining the secrets of a Master Mason, whereby they might travel in foreign countries and receive Master's wages, entered into a horrid conspiracy to extort them from our Grand Master, Hiram Abiff, or take his life; but, reflecting with horror on the atrocity of the crime, twelve of them recanted; the other three persisted in their murderous designs.

Our Grand Master, Hiram Abiff, was slain at high twelve. It was his usual practice at that hour, while the craft were called from labor to refreshment, to enter into the

---

[78] M.M. historical lecture

unfinished "Sanctum Sanctorum, or Holy of Holies," of the Temple, and there offer up his adorations to the Deity, and draw his designs on the trestle-board.

The three Fellow Crafts who persisted in their murderous designs, knowing this to be his usual practice, placed themselves at the south, west, and east gates of the inner courts of the temple, and there awaited his return.

Our Grand Master, Hiram Abiff, having finished his usual exercises, attempted to retire by the south gate, when he was accosted by Jubela, who thrice demanded of him the secrets of a Master Mason, or the Master's word, and, on his being refused, gave him a blow with the twenty-four-inch gauge across his throat, upon which he fled and attempted to pass out at the west gate, where he was accosted by Jubelo, who, in like manner, demanded of him the secrets of a blaster Mason, or the Master's word, and, on his being refused, gave him a blow with the square across his breast, upon which he fled, and attempted to make his escape out at the east gate, where he was accosted by Jubelum, who, in like manner, thrice demanded the secrets of a Master Mason, or the Master's word, and, on his like refusal, gave him a violent blow with the setting-maul on his forehead, which felled him dead on the spot.

The ruffians buried the body in the rubbish of the Temple until low-twelve, or twelve at night, when they met by agreement and carried it a westerly course from the Temple, to the brow of a hill west of Mount Moriah, where they buried it in a grave dug due east and west, six feet, perpendicular, at the head of which they planted an acacia, in order to conceal it, and that the place might be known, should occasion ever require, and made their escape.

Our Grand Master, Hiram Abiff, was found to be missing on the following day; his absence was discovered by there being no designs drawn on the trestle-board.

King Solomon, believing him to be indisposed, ordered strict search and due inquiry to be made for him through the several apartments of the Temple, that he might be found, if possible. But nothing could be seen or heard of him.

Then, fearing some accident had befallen him, the king ordered the several rolls of the workmen to be called, and there appeared to be three missing, namely: Jubela, Jubelo, and Jubelum, who, from the similarity of their names, were supposed to be brothers and men from Tyre.

About this time, the twelve Fellow Crafts, who had recanted from their murderous designs, appeared before King Solomon, clothed in white gloves and aprons, in token of their innocence, acknowledging their premeditated guilt, and, kneeling, implored his pardon.

King Solomon then ordered them to divide themselves into parties, and travel three east, three west, three north, and three south, and that they should, with others whom he should appoint, go in search of the ruffians.

The three that pursued a westerly course, coming down near the port of Joppa, met with a seafaring man, of whom they made inquiry, if he had seen any strangers pass that way; he informed them that he had, three, who, from them appearance, were workmen from the Temple, seeking a passage into Ethiopia, but not having King Solomon's pass, were not allowed to obtain one, and had returned back into the country.

They returned and bore this information to King Solomon, who ordered them to disguise themselves and travel as before, with positive instructions to find the ruffians and with as positive assurance that, if they did not, they twelve should he deemed the murderers, and suffer severely for the crime committed.

They travelled as before, and after fifteen days of weary travel and hardships, one of the brethren, being wearier than the rest, sat down on the brow of a hill, west of Mount Moriah, to rest and refresh himself, and, on attempting to rise, caught hold of an acacia, which easily giving way, excited his curiosity: upon examination they found it to be a grave.

At about this time a party arrived with the ruffians, and related that while sitting down to rest and refresh themselves, they heard the following horrid exclamations from the clefts of an adjacent rock.

The first was the voice of Jubela, exclaiming:

"Oh! that my throat had been cut across," &c., &c.

The second was the voice of Jubelo, exclaiming:

"Oh! that my body had been cut in two," &c., &c.

The third was the voice of Jubelum, exclaiming:

"Oh! that my body had been cut in two," &c., &c.

Upon which they rushed in, seized, bound, and brought them before King Solomon, who, after a due conviction of their guilt, ordered them to be taken without the gates of the courts of the Temple, and executed according to the several imprecations upon their own heads.

King Solomon then ordered the twelve Fellow Crafts to go in search of the body, and, if found, to observe whether the master's word, or a key to it, or anything appertaining to the Master's Degree, was on or about it.

The body of our Grand Master, Hiram Abiff, was found in a westerly course from the Temple, where our weary brothers sat down to rest and refresh themselves.

On removal of the earth, they came to the body of our Grand Master, Hiram Abiff, which they found in a high state of putrefaction, and in a mutilated and mangled condition, it having been buried already fifteen days: the effluvia which arose from it compelled them to place involuntarily their hands thus (Master here places his hands in form of a duegard of a Master Mason, which alludes to the manner in which his hands were placed when he took the oath of a Master Mason), to guard their nostrils--but nothing was found on or about the body excepting the jewel of his office, by which his body was easily discovered.

King Solomon then ordered them to go and assist in raising the body; and it was agreed between him and Hiram, king of Tyre, that as the master's word was then lost, the first sigh given at the grave, and the first word spoken after the body should be raised, should be used for the regulation of all Masters'

Lodges, until future generations find the right one.

They repaired to the grave, when King Solomon ordered one of the Fellow Crafts to take the body by the Entered Apprentice grip, and see if it could be raised; but, on account of its high state of decomposition, it could not be raised--the flesh cleaved from the bone.

King Solomon then ordered them to take it by the Fellow Craft grip; but on trial, for the reason before given, the Fellow Craft's grip failed to benefit any--it could not be raised.

King Solomon then exclaimed:

"O Lord my God, I fear the master's word is forever lost!
My brother of Tyre, what shall we do? Let us pray."
After prayer, King Solomon took the body by the strong grip of a Master Mason, or lion's paw, and raised it on the five points of fellowship, which have been explained to you. The body was then carried to the Temple for a more decent burial and was interred in due form.

The body of our Grand Master was buried three times: first, in the rubbish of the Temple; secondly, on the brow of a hill west of Mount Moriah; and, thirdly and lastly, as near the "Sanctum Sanctorum, or Holy of Holies," of King Solomon's Temple, as the Jewish law would permit; and Masonic tradition informs us that there was erected to his memory a Masonic monument, consisting of "a beautiful virgin, weeping over a broken column; before her was a book open; in her right hand a sprig of acacia, in her left an urn; behind her stands Time, unfolding and counting the, ringlets of her hair."

The beautiful virgin weeping over the broken column denotes the unfinished state of the Temple, likewise the untimely death of our Grand Master, Hiram Abiff; the book open before her, that his virtues lay on perpetual record; the sprig of acacia in her right hand, the divinity of the body; the urn in her left, that his ashes were therein safely deposited, under the "Sanctum Sanctorum, or Holy of Holies," of King Solomon's Temple.

Time, unfolding the ringlets of her hair, denoted that time, patience, and perseverance accomplish all things.

The Master now gives and explains to the candidate the several signs and tokens of this Degree, commencing with the first (see Figs. 5, 6, and 7, pages 17 and 18) and ending with the grips. (See Figs. 16 and 17, pages 97 and 120; also see Note L, Appendix.)

The Master next calls the candidate's attention to the three grand Masonic pillars, usually delineated on master's carpet (a Master's carpet is a large map that Lodges generally, keep, which is highly embellished with Masonic emblems).

Master, pointing to these pillars, says: "These are called the three grand Masonic columns or pillars, and are designated Wisdom, Strength, and Beauty.

"The pillar of Wisdom represents Solomon, King of Israel, whose wisdom contrived the mighty fabric; the pillar of Strength, Hiram, king of Tyre, who strengthened Solomon in his grand undertaking; the pillar of Beauty, Hiram Abiff, the widow's son, whose cunning craft and curious workmanship beautified and adorned the Temple.

"The construction of this grand edifice was attended with two remarkable circumstances. From Josephus we learn, that although seven years were occupied in building it, yet, during the whole time, it rained not in the daytime, that the workmen might not be obstructed in their labor, and from sacred history it appears that there was neither the sound of hammer, nor axe, nor any tool of iron, heard in the house while it was building. This famous fabric was supported by fourteen hundred and fifty-three columns, and two thousand nine hundred and six pilasters--all hewn from the finest Parian marble.

"There were employed in its building three Grand Masters; three thousand three hundred Masters, or overseers of the work; eighty thousand Fellow Crafts, or hewers on the mountains and in the quarries; and seventy thousand Entered Apprentices, or bearers of burdens. All these were, classed and arranged in such a manner, by the wisdom of Solomon, that neither envy, discord, nor confusion was suffered to interrupt that universal peace and tranquility which pervaded the world at that important period."

"Candidate, seven constitute a Lodge of Entered Apprentices--one Master Mason, and six Entered Apprentices. They usually meet on the Ground Floor of King Solomon's Temple.

"Five constitute a Lodge of Fellow Crafts two Master Masons and three Fellow Crafts. They usually meet in the Middle Chamber of King Solomon's Temple.

"Three constitute a Lodge of Master Masons--three Master Masons. They meet in the Sanctum Sanctorum, or Holy of Holies of King Solomon's Temple."

The Master either reads or repeats the following from a Monitor, which by many is committed to memory; but when he has the "work" (i.e., that part which is not monitorial), it is not necessary that he should commit to memory what is called the Master's carpet of emblems, but as it is a part of the initiation of the Third Degree, the author proposes to give it in its regular order of Lodge business.

GROUND FLOOR · MIDDLE CHAMBER · SANCTUM SANCTORUM

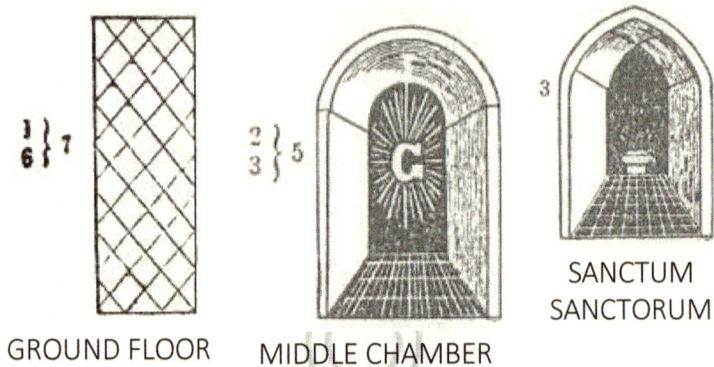

THE THREE STEPS

Usually delineated upon the master's carpet, are
emblematical of the three principal stages of human life,

viz.: youth, manhood, and age. In youth, in Entered Apprentices,

we ought industriously to occupy our minds in the attainment of useful knowledge; in manhood, as Fellow Crafts, we should apply our knowledge to the discharge of our respective duties to God, our neighbors, and ourselves; so that in age, as Master Masons, we may enjoy the happy reflections consequent on a well-spent life and die in the hope of a glorious immortality.

THE POT OF INCENSE

Is an emblem of a pure heart, which is always an acceptable sacrifice to the Deity; and as this glow with fervent heat, so should our hearts continually glow with gratitude to the great and beneficent Author of our existence, for the manifold blessings and comforts we enjoy.

THE BEEHIVE

Is an emblem of industry and recommends the practice of that virtue to all created beings, from the highest seraph in heaven to the lowest reptile of the dust. It teaches us that, as we come into the world rational and intelligent beings, so we should ever be industrious ones; never sitting down contented while our fellow creatures around us are in want, when it is in our power to relieve them without inconvenience to ourselves.

When we take a survey of nature, we view man, in his infancy, more helpless and indigent than the brute creation; he lies languishing for days, months, and years, incapable of providing sustenance for himself, of guarding against the attack of the wild beasts of the forest or sheltering himself from the in-clemencies of the weather.

It might have pleased the great Creator of heaven and earth to have made man independent of all other beings; but, as dependence is one of the strongest bonds of society, mankind was made dependent on each other for protection and security, as they thereby enjoy better opportunities of fulfilling the duties of reciprocal love and friendship. Thus was man formed for social and active life, the noblest part of the work of God; and he that will so demean himself as not to be endeavoring to add to the common stock of knowledge and understanding, may be deemed a drone In the hive of nature, a useless member of society, and unworthy of our protection as Masons.

THE BOOK OF CONSTITUTIONS, GUARDED BY THE TYLER'S SWORD,

Reminds us that we should be ever watchful and guarded in our thoughts, words, and actions, particularly when before the enemies of Masonry; ever bearing in remembrance those truly masonic virtues, silence, and circumspection.

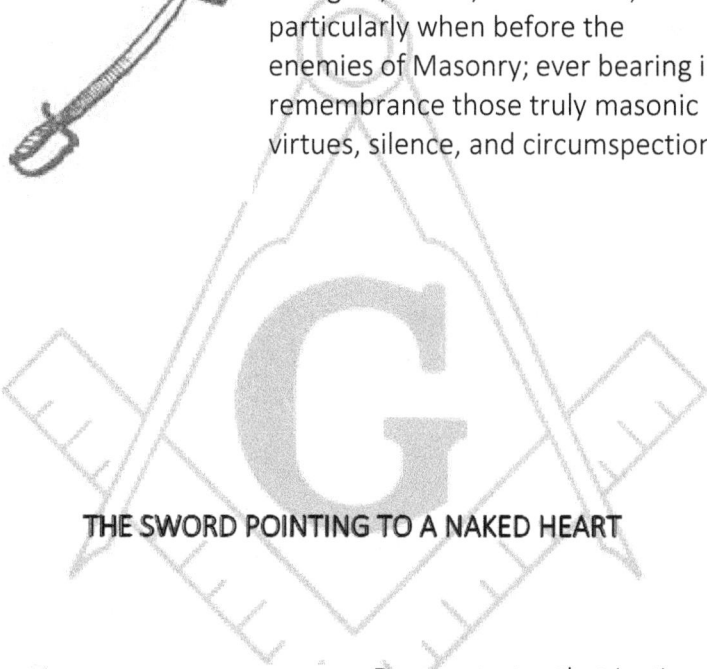

THE SWORD POINTING TO A NAKED HEART

Demonstrates that justice will eventually overtake us; and although us thoughts, words, and actions may be hidden from the eyes of man, yet that

ALL SEEING EYE!

whom the sun, moon, and stars obey, and under whose watchful care even comets perform their stupendous revolutions, beholds the inmost recesses of the human heart, and will reward us according to our works.

THE ANCHOR AND ARK

Are emblems of a well-grounded hope and a well-spent life. They are emblematical of that divine ark which safely bears us over this tempestuous sea of troubles, and that anchor

which shall safely moor us in a peaceful harbor, where the wicked cease from troubling, and the weary shall find rest.

THE FORTY-SEVENTH PROBLEM OF EUCLID.

This was an invention of our ancient friend and brother, the great Pythagoras, who, in his travels through Asia, Africa, and

Europe was initiated into several orders of priesthood and raised to the sublime degree of a Master Mason. This wise philosopher enriched his mind abundantly in a general knowledge of things, and more especially in geometry or masonry. On this subject he drew out many problems and theorems, and, among the most distinguished he erected this, which in the joy of his heart he called "Eureka," In the Grecian language signifying, "I have found it; "and upon the discovery of which he is said to have sacrificed a hecatomb. It teaches Masons to be general lovers of the arts and sciences.

THE HOUR-GLASS

Is an emblem of human life. Behold! how swiftly the sands run, and how rapidly our lives are drawing to a close. We cannot

without astonishment behold the little particles which are contained in this machine, how they pass away imperceptibly, and yet, to our surprise, in the short space of an hour they are all exhausted. Thus, wastes man! To-day he puts forth the tender leaves of hope; to-morrow blossoms, and bears his blushing honors thick upon him, the next day comes a frost, which nips the shoot, and, when he thinks his greatness still aspiring, he falls, like autumn leaves, to enrich oar mother earth.

THE SCYTHE

Is an emblem of time, which cuts the brittle thread of life, and

launches us into eternity. Behold! what havoc the scythe of time makes among the human race: if by chance we should escape the numerous evils incident to childhood and youth, and with health and vigor arrive at the years of manhood, yet withal we must soon be cut down by the all-devouring scythe of time, and be gathered into the land where our fathers have gone before us.

Candidates permit me to call your attention to the last emblem on the carpet--the spade, setting-maul, coffin, grave, and sprig of acacia.

The spade, which dug the grave of our Grand Master, may soon dig ours; the setting-maul, which terminated his earthly existence, may be among the casualties which will, sooner or later, terminate ours; the coffin, which received his remains, may soon receive ours; the grave, that abode for the dead, may soon be our grave; the acacia (that evergreen which once marked the temporary resting-place of the illustrious dead), that bloomed and flourished at the head of our Grand Master's grave, and was the cause of its timely discovery, is an emblem of our faith in the immortality of the soul, which never! never--no, never dies.

COFFIN, GRAVE, AND ACACIA

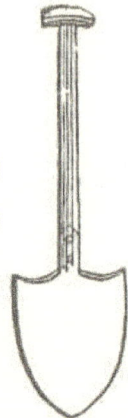

SETTING-MAUL

SPADE

This, my brother, may soon designate our last resting-place in that everlasting and silent abode, that haven of rest, that peaceful home, "where the wicked cease from troubling, and the weary are at rest."

Brother be ever mindful of that great change, when we shall be called from labors on earth to that everlasting refreshment in the paradise of God.

Let me admonish you, in the most serious manner, in reference to the close of life, that, when the cold winter of death shall have passed, and the bright summer morn of the resurrection appears, the Sun of Righteousness shall descend and send forth His angels to collect our ransomed dead; then, if we are found worthy, by the benefit of his "pass" we shall gain a ready admission into that celestial Lodge above, where the Supreme Architect of the Universe presides, where we shall see the King In the beauty of holiness, and with him enter into an endless eternity.

Some Masters add the following:

Thus, brother, we close our lecture on the emblems with the solemn thought of death. We are all born to die; we follow our friends to the brink of the grave, and, standing on the shore of a vast ocean, we gaze with exquisite anxiety until the last struggle is over, and we see them sink into the fathomless abyss. We feel our own feet sliding from the precarious brink on which We stand, and a few more suns, and we will be whelmed 'Neath death's awful wave, to rest in the stilly shades, and darkness Said silence will reign around our melancholy abode. But is this the end of man, and of the aspiring hopes of all faithful Masons?

No! blessed be God, we pause not our feet at the first or second step; but, true to our principles, look forward for greater light. As the embers of mortality are faintly glimmering in the sockets of existence, the Bible removes the dark cloud, draws aside the sable curtains of the tomb, bids hope and joy rouse us, and sustains and cheers the departing spirit; it points beyond the silent grave, and bids us turn our eyes with faith and confidence upon the opening scenes of our eternity.

The Worshipful Master gives three raps with his gavel, which brings the whole Lodge to their feet.

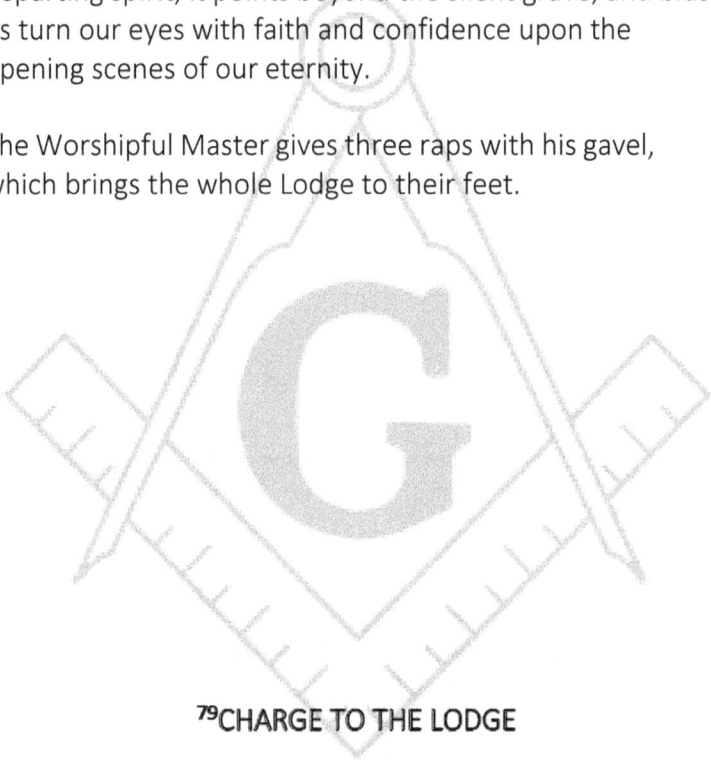

[79]CHARGE TO THE LODGE

And now, my brethren, let us see to it, and so regulate our lives by the plumb-line of justice, ever squaring our actions by the square of virtue, that when the Grand Warden of Heaven may call for us, we may be found ready; let us cultivate assiduously the noble tenets of our profession-- brotherly love, relief, and truth--and, from the square,

---

[79] The lodge is charged here

learn morality; from the level, equality; from the plumb, rectitude of life. Let us imitate, in all his various perfections, him who, when assailed by the murderous band of rebellious craftsmen, maintained his integrity, even in death, and sealed his pledge with his own blood. Let us emulate his amiable and virtuous conduct, his unfeigned piety to his God, his inflexible integrity to his trust; and as the evergreen that bloomed at the head of the grave be. took the place of his interment, so may virtue's ever-blooming loveliness designate us as free and accepted Masons. With the trowel, spread liberally the cement of brotherly love and affection; and, circumscribed by the compass, let us ponder well our words and actions, and let all the energies of our minds and the affections of our souls be employed in the attainment of our Supreme Grand Warden's approbation. Thus, when dissolution draws nigh, and the cold winds of death come sighing around us, and his chilly dews already glisten on our foreheads, with joy shall we obey the summons of the Grand Warden of Heaven and go from our labors on earth to everlasting refreshments in the Paradise of God. Then, by the benefit of the pass--a pure and blameless life--with a firm reliance on Divine Providence, shall we gain ready admission into that Celestial Lodge above, where the Supreme Grand Warden forever presides--forever reigns. When, placed at his right hand, he will be pleased to pronounce us just and upright Masons, then shall we be fitted as living stones for that spiritual temple, "that house not made with hands, eternal in the heavens," where no discordant voice shall be heard, but all the soul shall experience shall be perfect bliss, and all it shall express shall be perfect praise, and love divine shall ennoble every heart, and hallelujahs exalted employ every tongue.

The Master gives one rap with his gavel, when all take their seats except the candidate, who remains standing before the Master, by whom he is addressed as follows:

W. M.--Candidate, in closing this Degree, I now give you the following:

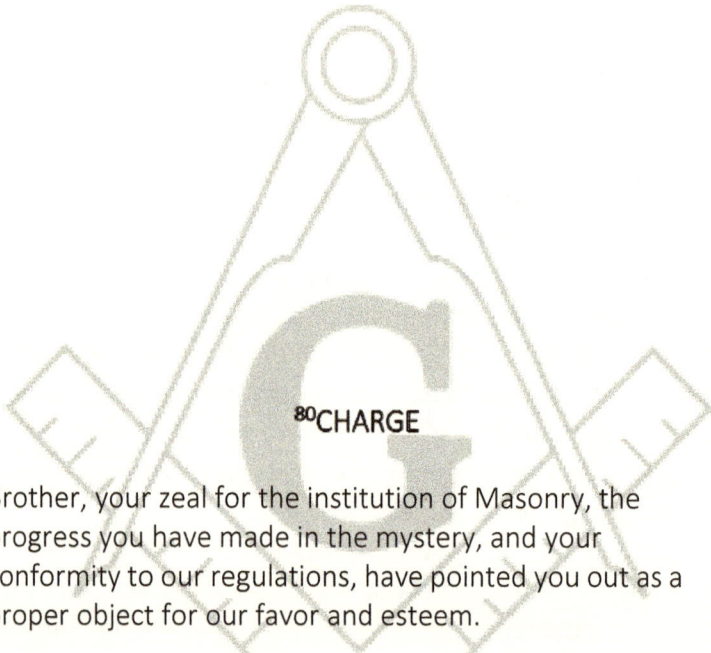

[80]CHARGE

Brother, your zeal for the institution of Masonry, the progress you have made in the mystery, and your conformity to our regulations, have pointed you out as a proper object for our favor and esteem.

You are now bound by duty, honor, and gratitude, to be faithful to your trust; to support the dignity of your character on every occasion; and to enforce, by precept and example, obedience to the tenets of the Order.

In the character of a Master Mason, you are authorized to correct the errors and irregularities of your uninformed brethren, and to guard them against a breach of fidelity.

---

[80] The candidate is charged here

To preserve the reputation of the fraternity unsullied must be your constant care; and, for this purpose, it is your province to recommend to your inferiors' obedience and submission; to your equals, courtesy, and affability; to your superiors, kindness, and condescension. Universal benevolence you are always to cultivate; and, by the regularity of your own behavior, afford the best example for the conduct of others less informed. The ancient landmarks of the order, entrusted to your care, you are carefully to preserve; and never suffer them to be infringed, or countenance a deviation from the established usages and customs of the fraternity.

Your virtue, honor, and reputation are concerned in supporting with dignity the character you now bear. Let no motive, therefore, make you swerve from your duty, violate your vows, or betray your trust; but be true and faithful, and imitate the example of that celebrated artist whom you this evening represent. Thus, you will render yourself deserving of the honor which we have conferred and merit the confidence we have reposed.

W. M.--Candidate, you will now take your seat in this Lodge as a Master Mason, after stepping to the Secretary's desk, and signing your name to the constitution and by-laws-- which will then make you a member of this Lodge.

There is a lecture to this Degree, as well as in the other Degrees, but it is not given by the Master to the candidate on the night of his "raising." The candidate gets this from some of the brethren who are well posted in the work. This Degree is very lengthy, and to give the lecture at an initiation would take up too much of the night; but if there is time, the Master and Senior Warden usually go through with the first section before closing the Lodge, so that the candidate and brethren may become conversant with it. The lecture is as follows:

FIRST SECTION.

Q. Are you a Master Mason?

A. I am.

Q. What induced you to become a Master Mason?

A. In order that I might travel in foreign countries, work, and receive master's wages, being better enabled to support myself and family, and contribute to the relief of worthy distressed Master Masons, their widows, and orphans.

Q. What makes you a Master Mason?

A. My obligation.

Q. Where did you make a Master Mason?

A. In a regularly constituted Lodge of Masons.

Q. How were you prepared?

A. By being divested of all metals, neither naked nor clothed, barefoot nor shod, hoodwinked, with a cable-tow three times around my body, in which condition I was conducted to the door of the Lodge by a brother.

Q. Why did you have a cable-two three times around your body?

A. To signify that my duties and obligations become increasingly binding as I advance in Masonry.

Q. How did you get admission?

A. By three distinct knocks.

Q. To what do they allude?

A. To the three jewels of a Master Mason, which are friendship, morality, and brotherly love.

Q. What was said to you from within?

A. Who comes here?

Q. Your answer?

A. Brother A. B., who has been regularly initiated Entered Apprentice, passed to the Degree of Fellow Craft, and now wishes further light in Masonry, by being raised to the sublime Degree of a Master Mason.

Q. What were you then asked?

A. If it was of my own free-will and accord, if I was worthy and qualified, duly, and truly prepared, had made suitable proficiency in the preceding Degree, and was properly vouched for; all which being answered in the affirmative, I was asked by what further right or benefit I expected to gain admission.

Q. What followed?

A. I was directed to wait with patience until the Worshipful Master should be informed of my request, and his answer returned.

Q. What answer did he return?

A. Let him enter and be received in due form.

Q. How were you received?

A. On both points of the compasses, extending from my naked left to my right breast, which was to teach me that, as the most vital parts of man are contained within the breast, so the most excellent tenets of our institution are contained between the points of the compasses, which are, friendship, morality, and brotherly love.

Q. How were you then disposed of?

A. I was conducted three times around the Lodge, to the Junior Warden in the south, where the same questions were asked, and like answers returned as at the door.

Q. How did the Junior Warden dispose of you?

A. He directed me to the Senior Warden in the west, and he to the Worshipful Master in the east, where the same questions were asked, and like answers returned as before.

Q. How did the Worshipful Master dispose of you?

A. He ordered me to be returned to the Senior Warden in the west, who taught me to approach the east by three upright regular steps, my feet forming the angle of a perfect square, my body erect at the altar, before the Worshipful Master in the east.

Q. What did the Worshipful Master do with you?

A. He made me a Master Mason in due form.

Q. What was that due form?

A. Kneeling on both my naked knees, both hands resting on the Holy Bible, square, and compasses; in which due form I took the solemn oath of a Master Mason, which is as follows:

(Here give the obligation; but it is never required--being only a matter of form.)

Q. After the obligation, what were you asked?

A. What I most desired.

Q. Your answer?

A. Further light in Masonry.

Q. Did you receive it?

A. I did, by order of the Worshipful Master and the assistance of the brethren.

Q. On being brought to light, what did you discover more than you had heretofore discovered?

A. Both points of the compasses elevated above the square, which was to teach me never to lose sight of those truly Masonic virtues, which are friendship, morality, and brotherly love.

Q. What did you then discover?

A. The Worshipful Master approaching me from the east, under the duegard of a Master Mason, who, in token of further continuance of his brotherly love and favor, presented me with his right hand, and with it the pass and token of the pass of a Master Mason, and ordered me to arise and salute the Junior and Senior Wardens as such.

Q. After saluting the Wardens, what did you first discover?

A. The Worshipful Master, who ordered me to the Senior Warden in the west, who taught me how to wear my apron as a Master Mason.

Q. How should a Master Mason wear his apron?

A. With the flap and corners turned down, which is to distinguish him as a Master Mason, or an overseer of the work.

Q. After being taught to wear your apron as a Master Mason, how were you then disposed of?

A. I was conducted to the Worshipful Master in the east, who presented me with the working-tools of a Master Mason, which are all the implements of Masonry indiscriminately, but more especially the trowel.

Q. What is the use of these tools?

A. The trowel is an instrument made use of by operative Masons to spread the cement, which unites a building into one common mass; but we, as free and accepted Masons, are taught to make use of it for the more noble and glorious purpose of spreading the cement of brotherly love and affection, &c., &c. (See Monitor for the balance of this answer, or page 99 of this work.)

Q. How were you then disposed of?

A. I was ordered to be returned to the place from whence I came, and reinvested of what I had been divested of, and wait the Worshipful Master's will and pleasure.

SECOND SECTION.

Q. What does a Master's Lodge represent?

A. The unfinished Sanctum Sanctorum, or Holy of Holies, of King Solomon's Temple.

Q. Did you ever return to the Lodge?

A. I did.

Q. On your return to the Lodge, where were you placed?

A. In the center, where I was caused to kneel, and implore the blessings of Deity.

Q. After imploring the blessings of Deity, what followed?

A. I arose, and on my passage around the Lodge was accosted by three Fellow Crafts, who thrice demanded of me the secrets of a Master Mason; and, on being refused, the first gave me a blow with the twenty-four-inch gauge, across my throat; the second with a square, across my breast; the third with a setting-maul, on my forehead, which felled me on the spot.

Q. What did you then represent?

A. Our Grand Master, Hiram Abiff, who was slain just before the completion of King Solomon's Temple.

Q. Was his death premeditated?

A. It was, by fifteen Fellow Crafts, who, seeing the Temple about to be completed, and being desirous of obtaining the secrets of a Master Mason, whereby they might travel in foreign countries, work, and receive Master's wages, entered into a horrid conspiracy to extort them from our Grand Master, Hiram Abiff, or take his life; but, reflecting with horror on the atrocity of the crime, twelve of them recanted; the other three persisted in their murderous designs.

Q. At what hour was our Grand Master, Hiram Abiff, slain?
A. At high twelve.

Q. How did he come to be assassinated at that hour?

A. It was his usual practice at high twelve, while the Craft were called from labor to refreshment, to enter into the unfinished Sanctum Sanctorum, or Holy of Holies of the Temple, and there to offer up his adorations to Deity, and there to draw his designs on the trestle-board.

Q. Who was the murderers?

A. The three Fellow Crafts who persisted in their murderous designs, knowing this to be his usual practice, placed themselves at the south, west, and east gates of the inner courts of the Temple, and there awaited his return.

Q. What followed?

A. Our Grand Master, Hiram Abiff, having finished his usual exercises, attempted to retire at the south gate, where he was accosted by Jubela, who thrice demanded of him the secrets of a Master Mason, or the Master's word; and, on being refused, gave him a blow with the twenty-four-inch gauge across the throat, upon which he fled, and attempted to pass out at the west gate, where he was accosted by Jubelo, who, in like manner, thrice demanded of him the secrets of a Master Mason, or the Master's word; and, on his being refused, gave him a blow with a square across his breast, upon which he fled, and attempted to make his escape out at the east gate, where he was accosted by Jubelum, who, in like manner, thrice demanded of him the secrets of a Master .Mason, or the

Master's word: and, on his being refused, gave him a violent blow with a setting-maul, on his forehead, which felled him dead on the spot.

Q. What did they do with the body?

A. They buried it in the rubbish of the Temple until low twelve, or twelve at night, when they met by agreement and carried it a westerly course from the Temple, to the brow of a hill west of Mount Moriah, where they buried it in a grave dug due east and west, six feet perpendicular, at the head of which they planted an acacia, in order to conceal it, and that the place might be known, should occasion ever require; and then made their escape.

Q. When was our Grand Master, Hiram Abiff, found to be missing?

A. On the following day.

Q. How was his absence discovered?

A. By there being no designs drawn on the trestle-board.

Q. What followed?

A. King Solomon, being informed of this, supposed him to be indisposed, and ordered strict search to be made for him through the several apartments of the Temple, and due inquiry made; search and inquiry were accordingly made, but he could not be found.

Q. What followed?

A. King Solomon, fearing some accident had befallen him, ordered the several rolls of the workmen to be called; and, after rollcall, it was found that three Craftsmen were missing, namely, Jubela, Jubelo, and Jubelum, who, from the similarity of their names, were supposed to be brothers, and men from Tyre.

Q. What followed?

A. At this time, the twelve Fellow Crafts, who had recanted from their murderous designs, appeared before King Solomon, clothed in white gloves and aprons, in token of their innocence, acknowledging their premeditated guilt, and humbly imploring his pardon.

Q. What followed?

A. King Solomon ordered them to divide into parties, and travel three east, three west, three north, and three south, with others whom he should appoint, in search of the ruffians.

Q. What followed?

A. The three, as they were passing a westerly course, coming down near the port of Joppa, met a seafaring man, of whom they inquired if he had seen any strangers pass that way. He informed them that he had seen three, who, from their appearance, were workmen from the Temple, seeking a passage into Ethiopia; but, not having King

Solomon's passes were unable to obtain one, and had returned back into the country.

Q. What followed?

A. They returned and bore this intelligence to King Solomon, who ordered them to divide themselves, and travel as before, with positive instructions to find the ruffians, and with as positive assurance, that if they did not the twelve should be deemed the murderers and suffer severely for the crime committed.

Q. What followed?

A. They travelled as before, and, after many days of hardships and toil, on their return one of the brethren, more weary than the rest, sat down on the brow of a hill to rest and refresh himself, and on attempting to rise, accidentally caught hold of an acacia, which easily giving way, aroused his curiosity; upon which he hailed his companions, and on examination found it to be a grave.

Q. What followed?

A. At this time a party arrived with the ruffians, and related that, while sitting down to rest and refresh themselves, they heard the following horrid exclamations from the clefts of an adjacent rock: the first was the voice of Jubela, exclaiming, "Oh! that my throat had been cut across," &c., &c.; the second was the voice of Jubelo, exclaiming, "Oh! that my breast had been torn open." &c., &c.; the third was the voice of Jubelum, exclaiming, "Oh! that my body had been severed in two, my bowels taken from thence. Upon which they rushed in, seized, bound, and brought them before King Solomon, who, after due conviction of their guilt, ordered them to be executed according to their several imprecations upon their own heads, uttered from the clefts of the rocks.

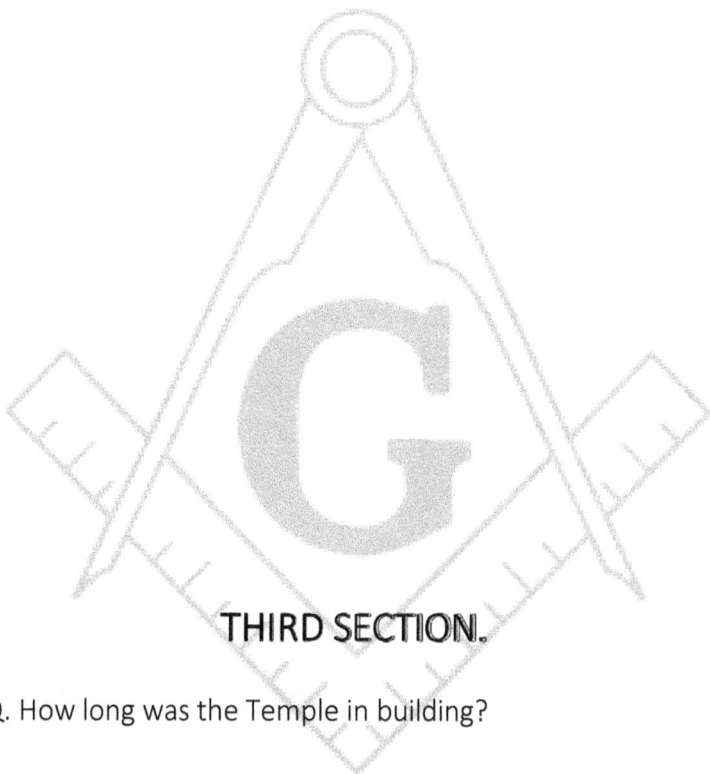

THIRD SECTION.

Q. How long was the Temple in building?

A. Seven years; during which it rained not in the daytime, that the workmen might not be obstructed in their labor.

Q. What supported the Temple?

A. Fourteen hundred and fifty-three columns, and two thousand nine hundred and six pilasters; all hewn from the finest Parian marble.

Q. What further supported it?

A. Three grand columns or pillars.

Q. What were they called?

A. Wisdom, Strength, and Beauty.

Q. What did they represent?

A. The pillar of Wisdom represented Solomon, king of Israel, whose wisdom contrived the mighty fabric; the pillar of strength, Hiram, king of Tyre, who strengthened Solomon in his grand undertaking; the pillar of Beauty, Hiram Abiff, the widow's son, whose cunning craft, and curious workmanship beautified and adorned the Temple.

Q. How many were there employed in the building of King Solomon's Temple?

A. Three Grand Masters, three thousand three hundred Masters or overseers of the work, eighty thousand Fellow Crafts, and seventy thousand Entered Apprentices.

Q. How many constitute an Entered Apprentices' Lodge?

A. Seven; one Master and six Entered Apprentices.

Q. Where did they usually meet?

A. On the Ground Floor of King Solomon's Temple.

Q. How many constitute a Fellow Crafts' Lodge?

A. Five; two master's and three Fellow Crafts.

Q. Where did they usually meet?

A. In the Middle Chamber of King Solomon's Temple.

Q. How many constitute a Masters' Lodge?

A. Three Master Masons.

Q. Where did they usually meet?

A. In the Sanctum Sanctorum, or Holy of Holies, of King Solomon's Temple.

Q. Have you any emblems in this Degree?

A. We have several, and they are divided into two classes.

Q. What is the first class?

A. The Pot of Incense, the Beehive, the Book of Constitutions guarded by Tyler's Sword, the Sword pointing to a Naked Heart, the All-seeing Eye, the Anchor and Ark, the Forty-seventh Problem of Euclid, the Hourglass, the Scythe, and the Three Steps on the master's Carpet.

Q. How are they explained?

These answers are monitorial.

Q. What are the second class of emblems?

A. The Setting-Maul, Spade, Coffin, Grave, and Sprig of Acacia; and are thus explained.

Reader, I have given you the whole of the first three Degrees in Masonry. This ends the third, or Master Masons' Degree.

But few Masons take sufficient interest in Masonry to be advanced further, and consequently do not get the password which was lost by the tragical death of Hiram Abiff.

King Solomon is said to have substituted, in place of the lost one, the word now used in the Master Masons' Degree, viz.: Mah-Hah-Bone, which is given on the five points of fellowship, and in low breath.

The missing word was found, after four hundred and seventy years, and was then, and still is, used in the Royal Arch Degree, as will be seen in the ceremonies of that Degree.

CLOSING THE LODGE.

The Lodge is closed in the same manner that it is opened, and, in fact, all three of the Degrees are closed alike.

We will suppose the business of the Lodge finished, and that the Master proceeds to close.

W. M.--Brother Senior Warden, do you know of anything further before this Lodge of Masons previous to closing?

S. W. (rising to his feet, and giving the sign of a Master Mason, if opened on that Degree.)--Nothing, Worshipful (some say), in the west. (Sits down.)

W. M.--Anything in the south, Brother Junior Warden?

J. W. (makes the same sign as the Senior Warden.)-- Nothing, Worshipful.

W. M.--Brother Secretary, have you anything on your desk?

Sec.--Nothing, Worshipful.

W. M.--Has any brother around the Lodge anything to offer for the benefit of Masonry before we proceed to close?

W. M.--Reading of the present communication.

W. M.--Brother Senior Warden, have you any alterations or additions to make to the minutes?

S. W. (rising to his feet and making the sign.) --I have none, Worshipful.

W. M.--Brother Junior Warden, have you any to make?

J. W.--None, Worshipful.

W. M.--Has any brother present any?

W. M.--Brethren, the minutes will stand approved, if there are no objections. (Gives one rap (•), when the Junior Deacon, at the inner door of the Lodge, rises to his feet.) Brother Junior Deacon, the last as well as the first care of Masons, when convened?

J. D. (makes sign.) --To see that the Lodge is duly tiled.

W. M.--You will address that part of your duty and inform the Tyler that we are about to close this Lodge and direct him to tyle accordingly. (Deacon opens the door and delivers his message.)

J. D.--The Lodge is titled, Worshipful.

W. M.--How tyled?

J. D.--By a brother of this Degree within the outer door.

W. M.--His duty there?

J. D.--To keep off all cowans and eavesdroppers, and suffer none to pass or repass, except such as are duly qualified and have the Worshipful Master's permission. (Sits down.)

W. M. (one rap, Senior Warden rises to his feet.) --Brother Senior Warden, at the opening of this Lodge you informed me that you were a Master Mason. What induced you to become a Master Mason?

S. W.--In order that I might travel in foreign countries, work, and receive master's wages, being better enabled to support myself and family, and contribute to the relief of worthy distressed Master Masons, their widows, and orphans.

W. M.--Have you ever travelled?

S. W.--I have, from west to east, and from east to west again. Some Lodges use the following questions and answers, both at opening and closing:

W. M.--Why did you leave the west and travel to the east?

S. W.--In search of that which was lost.

W. M.--To what do you allude, my brother?

S. W.--The Master's word.

W. M.--Did you find it?

S. W.--I did not but found a substitute.

W. M.--The Junior Deacon's station?

S. W.--At the right hand of the Senior Warden in the west.

W. M. (two raps, all the officers rise to their feet.) --Your duty there, Brother Junior Deacon?

J. D.--(See opening ceremony, p. 14.)

W. M.--The Senior Deacon's station?

J. D.--At the right hand of the Worshipful Master in the east.

W. M.--Your duty there, Brother Senior Deacon?

S. D.--(See opening ceremony, p. 14.)

W. M.--The Secretary's station?

S. D.--At the left hand of the Worshipful Master in the east.

W. M.--Your duty there, Brother Secretary?

W. M.--The Treasurer's station?

S. D.--At the left hand of the Worshipful Master in the east.

W. M.--Your duty there, Brother Treasurer?

Treasurer--(See opening ceremony, p. 14.)

W. M.--The Junior Warden's station?

Treasurer--In the south, Worshipful.

W. M.--Why in the south, and your duty there, Brother Junior?

J. W.--(See opening ceremony, p. 15.)

W. M.--The Senior Warden's station?

J. W.--In the west, Worshipful Master.

W. M.-- Why in the west, and your duty there, Brother Senior?

S. W.--(See opening ceremony, p. 15.)

W. M.--The Worshipful Master's station?

S. W.--In the east, Worshipful.

W. M.--Why in the east, and his duty there?

S. W.--As the sun rises in the east, to open and govern the day, so rises the Worshipful Master in the east (here the Master gives three raps (• • •), when all in the Lodge rise to their feet, the Master rising first), to open and govern his Lodge, set the Craft to work, and give them proper instructions.

W. M.--Brother Senior Warden, it is my order that this Lodge be now closed and stand closed until our next regular communication (barring emergency), when all, or a suitable number, shall have due and timely notice. In the meantime, it is hoped and expected that every brother will demean himself as becomes a man and a Mason. This you will communicate to the Junior Warden in the south, and he to the brethren about the

Lodge, that they are having due and timely notice, may govern themselves accordingly.

S. W.--Brother Junior Warden, it is the orders of the Worshipful Master, &c., &c.

J. W.--Brethren, you have heard the orders of the Worshipful Master, as communicated to me through the Senior Warden in the west--you will take notice and govern yourselves accordingly.

W. M.--Brethren, together on the signs. (The signs are just the same as at opening. See pp. 16, 17, 18; also p. 155.)

After the signs are gone through with by the whole Lodge, the Master gives one rap with his gavel, which is responded to by the Senior Warden, and then by the Junior Warden, and then again by the Master, one rap. Senior Warden, one. Junior Warden, one. Again, the Master, one. Senior Warden, one. Junior Warden, one. Rapping three times each.

W. M.--Brother Senior Warden, how should Masons meet?

S. W.--On the Level.

W. M.--And how does Brother Junior?

J. W.--On the Plumb.

W. M.--And part on the Square; and so, let us ever meet, act, and part.

Master takes off his hat, and repeats the following prayer:

"May the blessing of Heaven rest upon us, and all regular Masons; may brotherly love prevail, and every moral and social virtue cement us. Amen."

Response--So mote it be.

Some Lodges sing the following, to the air of "Bonny Doon";

"Adieu! a heart-warm, fond adieu,
   Ye brothers of our mystic tie,
Ye favored and enlightened few,
Companions of my social joy."

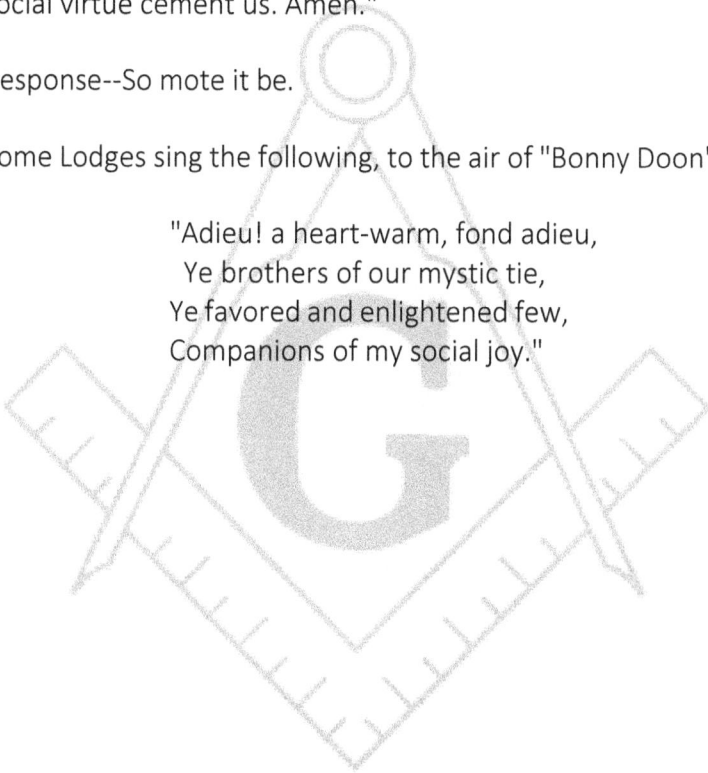

[81]CHARGE AT CLOSING A LODGE

BRETHREN: --You are now about to quit this sacred retreat of friendship and virtue, to mix again with the world. Amid its concerns and temptations, forget not the duties you have heard so frequently inculcated and so forcibly recommended in this Lodge. Be diligent, prudent, temperate, discreet. Remember that you have promised to befriend and relieve every brother who shall need your assistance; you have promised to remind him, in the friendliest manner, of his errors, and, if possible, to aid him in a reformation. These generous principles are to extend further. Every human being has a claim upon your kind offices. Do good unto all. Remember it more "especially to the household of the faithful."

Finally, brethren, be ye all of one mind, live in peace, and may the God of love and peace delight to dwell with and bless you.

W. M.--Brother Senior Warden, I now declare this Lodge duly closed. Brother Junior Deacon (turning to that officer), you will inform Tyler.

---

[81] The lodge is closed

"Words are potent weapons for all causes, good or bad." Manly P. Hall

www.ingramcontent.com/pod-product-compliance
Lightning Source LLC
Chambersburg PA
CBHW021222090426
42740CB00006B/344